Margaret Mead

Margaret Mead

EDRA ZIESK

CHELSEA HOUSE PUBLISHERS

NEW YORK · PHILADELPHIA

Chelsea House Publishers
EDITOR-IN-CHIEF Nancy Toff
EXECUTIVE EDITOR Remmel T. Nunn
MANAGING EDITOR Karyn Gullen Browne
COPY CHIEF Juliann Barbato
PICTURE EDITOR Adrian G. Allen
ART DIRECTOR Maria Epes
MANUFACTURING MANAGER Gerald Levine

American Women of Achievement
SENIOR EDITOR Constance Jones

Staff for MARGARET MEAD
TEXT EDITOR Marian W. Taylor
COPY EDITOR Mark Rifkin
DEPUTY COPY CHIEF Nicole Bowen
EDITORIAL ASSISTANT Claire Wilson
PICTURE RESEARCHER Patricia Burns
ASSISTANT ART DIRECTOR Loraine Machlin
DESIGNER Debora Smith
LAYOUT Ghila Krajzman
PRODUCTION COORDINATOR Joseph Romano
COVER ART Daniel Mark Duffy
COVER ORNAMENT Sarah Lewis

7 9 8 6

Library of Congress Cataloging-in-Publication Data

Ziesk, Edra.
   Margaret Mead / Edra Ziesk.

      p.   cm.—(American women of achievement)
   Summary: A biography of the now legendary anthropologist
famous for her studies of primitive cultures.
   ISBN 1-55546-667-2
      0-7910-0443-0 (pbk.)
   1. Mead, Margaret, 1901–1978—Juvenile
literature.   2. Anthropologists—United States—Biography—
Juvenile literature.   3. Ethnology—Melanesia—Juvenile
literature.   4. Melanesia—Social life and customs—
Juvenile literature. [1. Mead, Margaret, 1901–1978.
2. Anthropologists.] I. Title. II. Series.
GN21.M36Z54   1990
306'.092—dc20   89-17466
[B]   CIP
[92]   AC

CONTENTS

"Remember the Ladies"—Matina S. Horner   7

1. "A World All and Always Beautiful"   13

2. Coming of Age in Pennsylvania   23

3. Ash Can Cat   33

4. Fieldwork and Fame   47

5. "Sex and Temperament"   59

6. Bali   71

7. Culture and Change   81

8. Becoming a Legend   91

Further Reading   104

Chronology   105

Index   106

AMERICAN WOMEN OF ACHIEVEMENT

Abigail Adams
women's rights advocate

Jane Addams
social worker

Louisa May Alcott
author

Marian Anderson
singer

Susan B. Anthony
woman suffragist

Ethel Barrymore
actress

Clara Barton
founder of the American Red Cross

Elizabeth Blackwell
physician

Nellie Bly
journalist

Margaret Bourke-White
photographer

Pearl Buck
author

Rachel Carson
biologist and author

Mary Cassatt
artist

Agnes de Mille
choreographer

Emily Dickinson
poet

Isadora Duncan
dancer

Amelia Earhart
aviator

Mary Baker Eddy
founder of the Christian Science church

Betty Friedan
feminist

Althea Gibson
tennis champion

Emma Goldman
political activist

Helen Hayes
actress

Lillian Hellman
playwright

Katharine Hepburn
actress

Karen Horney
psychoanalyst

Anne Hutchinson
religious leader

Mahalia Jackson
gospel singer

Helen Keller
humanitarian

Jeane Kirkpatrick
diplomat

Emma Lazarus
poet

Clare Boothe Luce
author and diplomat

Barbara McClintock
biologist

Margaret Mead
anthropologist

Edna St. Vincent Millay
poet

Julia Morgan
architect

Grandma Moses
painter

Louise Nevelson
sculptor

Sandra Day O'Connor
Supreme Court justice

Georgia O'Keeffe
painter

Eleanor Roosevelt
diplomat and humanitarian

Wilma Rudolph
champion athlete

Florence Sabin
medical researcher

Beverly Sills
opera singer

Gertrude Stein
author

Gloria Steinem
feminist

Harriet Beecher Stowe
author and abolitionist

Mae West
entertainer

Edith Wharton
author

Phillis Wheatley
poet

Babe Didrikson Zaharias
champion athlete

CHELSEA HOUSE PUBLISHERS

"REMEMBER THE LADIES"

MATINA S. HORNER

Remember the Ladies." That is what Abigail Adams wrote to her husband, John, then a delegate to the Continental Congress, as the Founding Fathers met in Philadelphia to form a new nation in March of 1776. "Be more generous and favorable to them than your ancestors. Do not put such unlimited power in the hands of the Husbands. If particular care and attention is not paid to the Ladies," Abigail Adams warned, "we are determined to foment a Rebellion, and will not hold ourselves bound by any Laws in which we have no voice, or Representation."

The words of Abigail Adams, one of the earliest American advocates of women's rights, were prophetic. Because when we have not "remembered the ladies," they have, by their words and deeds, reminded us so forcefully of the omission that we cannot fail to remember them. For the history of American women is as interesting and varied as the history of our nation as a whole. American women have played an integral part in founding, settling, and building our country. Some we remember as remarkable women who—against great odds—achieved distinction in the public arena: Anne Hutchinson, who in the 17th century became a charismatic religious leader; Phillis Wheatley, an 18th-century black slave who became a poet; Susan B. Anthony, whose name is synonymous with the 19th-century women's rights movement and who led the struggle to enfranchise women; and, in our own century, Amelia Earhart, the first woman to cross the Atlantic Ocean by air.

These extraordinary women certainly merit our admiration, but other women, "common women," many of them all but forgotten, should also be recognized for their contributions to American thought and culture. Women have been community builders; they have founded schools and formed voluntary associations to help those in need; they have assumed the major responsibility for rearing children, passing on from one generation to the next the values that keep a culture alive. These and innumerable other contributions, once ignored, are now being recognized by scholars, students, and the public. It is exciting and gratifying to realize that a part of our history that was hardly acknowledged a few generations ago is now being studied and brought to light.

In recent decades, the field of women's history has grown from obscurity to a politically controversial splinter movement to academic respectability, in many cases mainstreamed into such traditional disciplines as history, economics, and psychology. Scholars of women, both female and male, have organized research centers at such prestigious institutions as Wellesley College, Stanford University, and the University of California. Other notable centers for women's studies are the Center for the American Woman and Politics at the Eagleton Institute of Politics at Rutgers University; the Henry A. Murray Research Center for the Study of Lives, at Radcliffe College; and the Women's Research and Education Institute, the research arm of the Congressional Caucus on Women's Issues. Other scholars and public figures have established archives and libraries, such as the Schlesinger Library on the History of Women in America, at Radcliffe College, and the Sophia Smith Collection, at Smith College, to collect and preserve the written and tangible legacies of women.

From the initial donation of the Women's Rights Collection in 1943, the Schlesinger Library grew to encompass vast collections documenting the manifold accomplishments of American women. Simultaneously, the women's movement in general and the academic discipline of women's studies in particular also began with a narrow definition and gradually expanded their mandate. Early causes such as woman suffrage and social reform, abolition and organized labor were joined by newer concerns such as the history of women in business and the professions and in politics and government; the study of the family; and social issues such as health policy and education.

Women, as historian Arthur M. Schlesinger, jr., once pointed out, "have constituted the most spectacular casualty of traditional history.

INTRODUCTION

They have made up at least half the human race, but you could never tell that by looking at the books historians write." The new breed of historians is remedying that omission. They have written books about immigrant women and about working-class women who struggled for survival in cities and about black women who met the challenges of life in rural areas. They are telling the stories of women who, despite the barriers of tradition and economics, became lawyers and doctors and public figures.

The women's studies movement has also led scholars to question traditional interpretations of their respective disciplines. For example, the study of war has traditionally been an exercise in military and political analysis, an examination of strategies planned and executed by men. But scholars of women's history have pointed out that wars have also been periods of tremendous change and even opportunity for women, because the very absence of men on the home front enabled them to expand their educational, economic, and professional activities and to assume leadership in their homes.

The early scholars of women's history showed a unique brand of courage in choosing to investigate new subjects and take new approaches to old ones. Often, like their subjects, they endured criticism and even ostracism by their academic colleagues. But their efforts have unquestionably been worthwhile, because with the publication of each new study and book another piece of the historical patchwork is sewn into place, revealing an increasingly comprehensive picture of the role of women in our rich and varied history.

Such books on groups of women are essential, but books that focus on the lives of individuals are equally indispensable. Biographies can be inspirational, offering their readers the example of people with vision who have looked outside themselves for their goals and have often struggled against great obstacles to achieve them. Marian Anderson, for instance, had to overcome racial bigotry in order to perfect her art and perform as a concert singer. Isadora Duncan defied the rules of classical dance to find true artistic freedom. Jane Addams had to break down society's notions of the proper role for women in order to create new social institutions, notably the settlement house. All of these women had to come to terms both with themselves and with the world in which they lived. Only then could they move ahead as pioneers in their chosen callings.

Biography can inspiré not only by adulation but also by realism. It helps us to see not only the qualities in others that we hope to emulate but also, perhaps, the weaknesses that made them "human." By helping us identify with the subject on a more personal level they help us to feel that we, too, can achieve such goals. We read about Eleanor Roosevelt, for example, who occupied a unique and seemingly enviable position as the wife of the president. Yet we can sympathize with her inner dilemma: an inherently shy woman who had to force herself to live a most public life in order to use her position to benefit others. We may not be able to imagine ourselves having the immense poetic talent of Emily Dickinson, but from her story we can understand the challenges faced by a creative woman who was expected to fulfill many family responsibilities. And though few of us will ever reach the level of athletic accomplishment displayed by Wilma Rudolph or Babe Zaharias, we can still appreciate their spirit, their overwhelming will to excel.

A biography is a multifaceted lens. It is first of all a magnification, the intimate examination of one particular life. But at the same time, it is a wide-angle lens, informing us about the world in which the subject lived. We come away from reading about one life knowing more about the social, political, and economic fabric of the time. It is for this reason, perhaps, that the great New England essayist Ralph Waldo Emerson wrote, in 1841, "There is properly no history: only biography." And it is also why biography, and particularly women's biography, will continue to fascinate writers and readers alike.

Margaret Mead

On her 1925–26 field trip to American Samoa, Margaret Mead immersed herself in the traditional culture of the island. Here, she wears native dress.

ONE

"A World All and Always Beautiful"

On a warm summer morning in 1925, Margaret Mead stood on a Philadelphia railroad platform waiting for the train to San Francisco. Her parents and her young husband, Luther Cressman, were there to see her off. The 23-year-old Mead was about to begin the first leg of a 9,000-mile rail and sea journey that would take her to the Pacific islands of Samoa.

She was leaving home with a camera, a typewriter, a suitcase packed with the wrong kind of clothing, and, she later confessed, "all the courage of almost complete ignorance." Mead hardly fit the description of a seasoned traveler. "I had never been aboard a ship," she recalled in 1977, "had never spoken a foreign language or stayed in a hotel by myself. In fact, I had never spent a day of my life alone." Nonetheless, as she boarded her train, her father noted with amazement that "she never looked back."

Mead's destination, Samoa, was celebrated for its tropical beauty. Nineteenth-century writer Robert Louis Stevenson called it "a world all and always beautiful," and poet Rupert Brooke had written, "If you ever miss me suddenly . . . you'll know that I've got sick for the full moon . . . and the palms against the morning . . . and that I've gone back."

But Margaret Mead was not traveling to Samoa to enjoy the islands' tropical scenery. She had recently received her Ph.D. in anthropology—the scientific study of humankind, especially its development, customs, and beliefs. She was going to Samoa to carry out the first fieldwork assignment of her career, studying adolescence in a Polynesian culture. Mead's youth and physique—she stood 5 feet 2½ inches tall and weighed 98 pounds—made her in some ways an ideal candidate to infiltrate a group of teenagers. On the other hand, her physical frailty caused all who knew her to worry that she might not be able to withstand the challenges ahead.

Mead's chosen career, anthropology, was a relatively young science in 1925. Those who went out into the field were not only learning about a particular people but were also helping to shape a new discipline. Unlike other scientists who had the luxury of using carefully tested methods when carrying out their inquiries, early anthropologists such as Mead had to make up their techniques as they went along. It was an exciting, and daunting, prospect. Years later Mead wryly remarked that "if young fieldworkers do not give up in despair, go mad, ruin their health, or die, they do, after a fashion, become anthropologists."

Her decision to join this select group of rugged anthropologists was propelled by a sense of urgency. "Even in remote parts of the world," she wrote in her autobiography, *Blackberry Winter*, "ways of life about which nothing was known were vanishing before the onslaught of modern civilization. The work of recording these unknown ways of life had to be done now—*now*—or they would be lost forever."

When Mead first proposed going to Samoa, the home of several endangered cultures, she had met with resistance. Columbia University professor Franz Boas, the pioneering anthropologist who was overseeing Mead's fieldwork, had encouraged her to stay in the United States and study Native Americans. Eventually, though, he had given in to his determined student. "You know that I myself am not very pleased with this idea of her going to the tropics for a long stay," Boas wrote a colleague. "It seems to my mind, however ... that it would be much worse to put obstacles in her way that prevented her from doing a piece of work on which she had set her heart, than to let her run a certain amount of risk."

Undaunted by the dangers ahead, Mead embarked on the long journey to Samoa. On August 31, 1925, a cross-country train ride and two sea voyages after leaving Philadelphia, she finally arrived at her destination. Her boat docked in Pago Pago, the capital of Tutuila, the largest of the American Samoan islands. Although she had succeeded in getting to Samoa, her troubles were just beginning.

She went through a difficult period of adjustment common to most anthropologists during their first weeks in the field. An intimidating array of tasks lay before her: She needed to learn the language, become familiar with new customs, adapt to a different diet, and immerse herself in a totally alien culture. "For my first two months," she recalled, "I found myself often saying under my breath, 'I can't do it . . .' One day I noticed I was no longer saying this in English but in Samoan and then I knew that I could."

Though anxious to set up shop in a suitable village and to justify the National Research Council's faith in her project, expressed in the form of a $150-a-month grant, Mead found herself stuck in Pago Pago for 6 long weeks. The council insisted on sending her checks by mail rather than advancing the funds to her before she left for Samoa, and the money did not arrive, as expected, on the first boat after Mead's. Since American boats arrived in Pago Pago only once every three weeks, she could not pay her hotel bill and had no choice but to stay put until the next boat arrived.

The hotel where Mead was staying had been the setting for British writer Somerset Maugham's exotic short story "Rain," a fact that initially captured her imagination. Maugham had described the hotel as a picturesque building with wide verandas and a roof made of corrugated iron. Mead, however, found the hotel old and ramshackle. She thought the food was "dreadful" and felt that the hotel cook, Fa'alavelave (the Samoan word for misfortune), had been aptly named.

The mail boat finally arrived with her grant money. Mead paid her hotel bill and moved on to Vaitogi, known as "the village of the Turtle and the Shark." According to local legend, an

Franz Boas was a pioneer in American anthropology. Rejecting previous anthropological practice, he encouraged his students to live among their subjects for months at a time.

15

Members of the royal family of Vaitongi, such as the chief's daughter (above), instructed Mead in Samoan etiquette. Mead was a guest of the chief's during her first weeks in Samoa.

old woman and a child, neglected by their relatives during a famine, had jumped into the sea there and changed into a turtle and a shark. The children of Vaitogi often stood on the shore and sang to summon the animals. Mead witnessed this ritual on her first day in the village, and to her surprise both a turtle and a shark appeared.

Mead spent 10 days as the guest of Vaitogi's chief, Ufuti. The visit was arranged so that she could immerse herself in the language and customs of the Samoan people before beginning her actual fieldwork. Mead adapted quickly. She learned to eat Samoan food, to recognize the plants used in weaving, and to practice correct Samoan etiquette, which included not talking when standing up inside a house and bending in a deep bow when passing a seated person of high social rank. She thanked banquet hosts by donning native costumes and performing native dances with them. Nonetheless, Mead remained something of an oddity in Vaitogi. She wrote that her daily visits to the village shower attracted "staring crowds of children and passing adults."

Returning to Pago Pago at the end of October, Mead began preparations to leave for Tau island, where she would live and do her fieldwork for the next six months. She had chosen Tau for its manageable size (8 by 11 miles) and because 3 of its 4 villages were quite close together, which would make her research easier. Each of these villages housed between 900 and 1,000 people,

many of them the adolescent girls that Mead planned to study.

In early November she moved into the only American household in Tau, the Luma village home of U.S. Navy pharmacist's mate Edward Holt. Living with the Holts, who ran a combination drugstore and infirmary for the islanders, struck Mead as a good compromise. "If I lived in a Samoan house with a Samoan family," Mead explained in a letter home, "I might conceivably get into a little more intimate touch with that particular family." But she reasoned that these advantages would be offset by "the nervewracking conditions of living with half a dozen people in the same room, in a house without walls, always sitting on the floor and sleeping in constant expectation of having a pig or a chicken thrust itself upon one's notice."

Mead used the back veranda of the Holts' medical dispensary as her living quarters. There she interviewed adolescent girls as well as adult "informants" in order to learn about them and their culture. The youths spoke freely, but the adults expected payment for their information. Taking tally, Mead found that in one 2-week period she gave away 100 envelopes, 200 sheets of paper, dozens of cigarettes, and countless matches, onions, and sewing needles in exchange for information.

The villagers of Tau soon learned that Mead possessed a typewriter and a camera, and it did not take long for them to begin asking her to use both on their behalf. "Fale wants me to type a love song he has written to his sweetheart," an exasperated Mead wrote friends back home. "Lila wants the address on her letter to her daughter typed. . . . And to crown it all . . . a request [came that] I go over to Faleasao in the bright morning sun on the hottest day we've ever had to take a picture of a corpse."

Mead's work was further hampered by a severe hurricane that hit the island on New Year's Day, 1926. Rain poured down, and the air became thick with flying sand, coconuts, and pieces of tin roofing. She and the Holts survived the storm by huddling in a four-by-five-foot cement water tank. They emerged to discover near-total devastation: The storm ruined the crops and toppled every house in the village, including the Holts'. In the wake of the hurricane, the villagers of Tau struggled to rebuild their lives and homes, and Mead worked to complete her inquiry into Samoan culture. She continued talking with, observing, and testing her subjects, working "as many hours a day as I could stay awake."

As time passed, the Samoan villagers came to accept Mead almost as one of their own, an attitude that pleased her personally—and benefited her fieldwork. She wandered freely about the island to collect data. She visited neighboring houses and sometimes went swimming or night fishing with the children, who called her Makelita, after one of their former queens.

Mead's methods seemed informal at times, but they were supported by

Mead used the back porch of a U.S. medical dispensary as her living quarters during her stay in Samoa. The dispensary was home to the only other Americans on the island.

painstaking research. She drew neighborhood maps and wrote character sketches of many of the islanders. In time, she completed a census of Luma village and charted the backgrounds of the adolescent girls she was studying, gathering facts about the size of their families, their parents' wealth and social status, and other details of the girls' households. Mead also focused on the teenagers' personalities, including their religious attitudes, friendships, and scores on tests—first developed by British anthropologist William Rivers—for intelligence, color naming, and memory. She also recorded each girl's sexual history.

Mead's hard work was often punctuated by the colorful events of island life. One day, for example, a ceremonial visiting party arrived from another village, and the young anthropologist paid a call on the visiting chief, a woman named Talala. Mead presented Talala, the only female chief in the Samoan islands, with four yards of calico as a gift. In return, Talala declared Mead a *taupou* (ceremonial princess) and named her Fuailelagi, which translates as "Flower-in-the-heavens."

Mead's taupou status paid off in her quest for new informants and illuminating experiences. Toward the end of her stay in Samoa, some of the residents of her adopted village journeyed to Fitiuta, an isolated community at the opposite end of the island. Mead, as a ceremonial princess, was invited along. Because of her position, she became the confidante of Fitiuta's high

priests and attended several feasts and rituals. The only drawback was that she was required to give long, flowery speeches at these events. Not only were her powers of eloquence taxed but she was also expected to deliver her remarks in fluent Samoan. She wrote her family and friends at home that these speeches were "no picnic."

Letter writing provided one of the few outlets for Mead's emotions, which ranged from elation to despair. "My accounts of life in family bulletins were fairly evenly balanced between pain and pleasure," Mead later remarked, "but in my letters to friends I laid such heavy stress on points of difficulty that [they] concluded I was having a hard and disappointing time. The truth was that I had no idea whether I was using the right methods. What were the right methods? There were no precedents to fall back on."

But the resourceful and brilliant Mead was setting her own precedents, which would be followed by other young anthropologists in the coming years. After living and working alongside the people of Tau island for nine months, she left Samoa in June 1926. Back in the United States, she transformed her data and impressions into a book entitled *Coming of Age in Samoa: A Psychological Study of Primitive Youth for Western Civilization*. This landmark volume, published in 1928, became a controversial best-seller and is still the most widely read book in the history of anthropology.

Margaret Mead's ground-breaking

The island of Samoa has long been noted for its tropical beauty. The 19th-century author Robert Louis Stevenson called it "a world all and always beautiful."

study of Samoan culture brought her the fame and admiration that would be hers for the rest of her life. *Coming of Age in Samoa* introduced millions of people to anthropology, which pleased Mead because she felt that the new science offered unique tools for survival in an increasingly complex world. Of her field subjects, she wrote that "even the small children were collaborators in an undertaking that transcended both me and them—the attempt to understand enough about culture so that all of us, equally members of humankind, can understand ourselves and take our future and the future of our descendants safely in our hands."

Born in 1901, Margaret Mead grew up in a progressive Pennsylvania household. This portrait shows the bright, unconventional girl in 1912.

T W O

Coming of Age in Pennsylvania

Margaret Mead was born into an unconventional Philadelphia family on December 16, 1901. Even her birth was unusual: At a time when most babies were born at home, Margaret was the first child to be delivered at Philadelphia's West Park Hospital. Her parents made the then novel decision to have a hospital delivery because they were unusual, scientifically oriented people. Her father was an economist; her mother, a student of sociology.

Margaret's parents, Edward Sherwood Mead and Emily Fogg Mead, had met in a class at the University of Chicago in 1896. Family legend has it that the first time Edward Mead saw Emily Fogg he marched across the lec-

ture room, took a seat beside her, and announced his intention to marry her. He got his wish four years later.

The Meads established a marriage based on shared values that drew the marriage together and set it apart from their neighbors. In turn-of-the-century America, their fondness for progressive ideals was quite rare. "In a sense," Margaret Mead later remarked of her childhood, "we were like a family of refugees, always a little at odds with and well in advance of the local customs."

Edward Mead was a professor at the University of Pennsylvania's Wharton School, where he spearheaded the development of business studies by founding the institution's Evening School. He was also the author of five books and many articles on the economy and related topics. Edward Mead prized facts and clarity but was capable, Margaret recalled, of absent-mindedly putting her shoes on the wrong feet as he helped her dress. According to one relative, Edward Mead had "no experience in any way of the real world. He knew facts and tables and statistics, but his humanness was lacking."

Emily Mead was warmer than her husband, but she, too, was hardly a traditional parent. Near the end of her life, Emily remarked that "Margaret wanted a little rosebud mother." Rather than a storybook homemaker, Emily was a bright, active woman who divided her time between running a household and pursuing a scientific career. Her chosen field was sociology, the study of human society and its development. During the years she raised her family she was the recipient of a Bryn Mawr College fellowship that enabled her to continue her studies.

Emily Mead made a comfortable home for the four of her five children who survived infancy: Margaret, the firstborn; Richard, born in 1904; Elizabeth, who arrived five years later; and Priscilla, born in 1911. (Katherine, born in 1907, died at the age of nine months.) Their mother was not a frivolous person, and she had little sense of humor or playfulness, Margaret recalled. Instead, Mrs. Mead expressed her devotion to her children by providing them with books to stimulate their minds and plenty of time and space to exercise their bodies and imaginations outdoors. Home, Margaret remembered, was a place "in which children were fed nutritionally, book salesmen and nuns collecting for charity were invited to lunch, other people's children were welcomed and treated as people."

Much of Emily Mead's time was devoted to social causes. She encouraged her offspring to play with children from different backgrounds so that they would not develop racial and class prejudices. She was also an ardent feminist who lobbied to help win the vote for women.

In many respects Emily Mead embodied feminist ideals. Aside from her political activism, she pursued mental and physical activities (such as house painting) that were traditionally considered "unfeminine." While Emily followed her own course, apparently without worrying about societal prejudices, her perceptive daughter could not help but notice how much her mother stood out. Young Margaret reflected on these qualities in a poem about her mother, which said in part: "She has a lady's hands, but marred / By other than a Lady's work; / All intricately traced and scarred / By little tasks she will not shirk."

Margaret had another strong female role model while she was growing up. Her grandmother, Martha Ramsay Mead, lived with Edward and Emily and helped them raise their four children. "Grandma," Margaret Mead later commented, "was the most decisive influence in my life. She had gone to college when this was a very unusual thing for a girl to do, she had a firm grasp of anything she paid attention to, she had married and had a child, and she had a career of her own." Martha Mead had been a schoolteacher and principal, and it was she who oversaw the education of her grandchildren.

Surprisingly, despite their commitment to intellectual pursuits, the Meads were skeptical about formal schooling. "My family," Mead later wrote, "deeply disapproved of any school that kept children chained to their desks, indoors, for long hours every day." Accordingly, the Mead children, Margaret included, did not spend very much time in the classroom. Before she reached high school age, Margaret's formal education consisted of only two years of kindergarten and one year of half days in the fourth grade.

Most of Margaret's education took place at home, in tutoring sessions with Grandma Mead. These lessons, which seldom lasted more than an hour a day, were supplemented by forays into the surrounding woods and fields. Years later, Mead praised her grandmother's methods: "She understood many things that are barely recognized in the wider educational world even today. She thought that memorizing mere facts was not very important and that drill was stultifying. The result was that I was not well drilled in geography or spelling. But I learned to observe the world around me and to note what I saw."

A young woman celebrates the ratification of the Nineteenth Amendment to the Constitution, which in 1920 gave women the right to vote. Mead's mother, Emily, took an active part in the suffrage movement.

Unlike most middle-class mothers of her time, Emily Fogg Mead encouraged her offspring to play with children from different backgrounds.

Emily Mead was also involved in her children's education. She sought out skilled artisans to teach them such crafts as wood carving, carpentry, basket making, and clay modeling. At one time Margaret received twice-weekly painting lessons. Her instructor was an illustrator of girls' books, and Margaret paid for her lessons by posing for him.

It was from her father that Margaret learned the difference between economic theory and the realities of day-to-day business. In some respects, Edward Mead was better versed in the former than the latter. He was constantly busy with experimental businesses that sometimes augmented the family's income but more often depleted it. One of his ongoing interests was researching possible uses for the waste products of coal mining, and he often used the Mead household as a testing ground. One winter, Margaret recalled, an experiment backfired, and their entire house "was filled with the smoke of great unbound hunks of coal dust."

The Meads moved often, mostly in and around Philadelphia. Margaret Mead once estimated that she had lived in 60 houses by the time she reached her early teens. In her earliest years, home during the spring and fall was a house with five acres in Hammonton, N.J., where Emily Mead did her doctoral research with Italian immigrant families. Summers were spent in the country, winters in or near Philadelphia, close to the university where her father worked.

Margaret's favorite residence was probably the Buckingham Valley, Pennsylvania, farm where the family moved when she was a preteen. The farm had 107 acres, with a brook, a windmill, grain fields, and a carriage house. The barn did double duty as a shelter for animals and a theater for plays the Mead children often presented. Wherever else the family moved, the farm was considered home until it was sold in 1928.

When she was 11 years old, Margaret had herself baptized in the Episcopalian

Edward Mead, a college professor, was a founder of the Wharton Evening School at the University of Pennsylvania. A talented theoretician, he was somewhat absentminded in daily life.

church. "I enjoyed prayer," Mead wrote in *Blackberry Winter.* "I enjoyed church. The other children I knew thought all of this was odd." So did her parents, who were not religious. Edward Mead, in particular, treated his eldest daughter's religious beliefs with sarcasm. As Margaret grew up, whenever her behavior displeased him, he would threaten to have Margaret "unbaptized," a joke the serious-minded youngster did not find funny.

Margaret's religious faith and her unusual family life set her apart from her peers. She later wrote that she had mixed feelings about her unconventional upbringing:

I took pride in being unlike other children and in living in a household that was itself unique. But at the same time I longed to share in every culturally normal experience. I wished that I had been born in a house. I wanted to have a locket, like other little girls, and to wear a hat with ribbons and fluffy petticoats instead of the sensible bloomers that very advanced mothers put on their little daughters so they could climb trees. . . . But I also wanted to be very sure that I would always be recognized as myself.

Nicknamed Punk by her father, Margaret was a headstrong and precocious child.

Certainly, even in her early childhood, Margaret was widely recognized as a formidable individual. Her father, who affectionately dubbed her Punk, had several favorite stories about his firstborn's strong character. One of them involved a visit to a Philadelphia park, where he pretended to abandon the unruly Margaret in order to frighten her into obeying him. According to *Blackberry Winter*, the headstrong three year old won the upper hand by loudly crying, "Bad Dada to go off and leave his poor little baby girl!" Her embarrassed father had no choice but to return and pick Margaret up in an attempt to appease "the condemnatory glances of other Sunday strollers." Because of this and other incidents, her family often remarked, sometimes in exasperation, "There is no one like Margaret."

In 1913, when the family moved to Doylestown, Pennsylvania, Margaret went to a "quite good" small-town high school. There, for the first time, she had teachers who were college graduates. As she neared adulthood, Mead began to consider her future. "At different times," she wrote, "I wanted to become a lawyer, a nun, a writer or a minister's wife with six children. Looking to my grandmother and my mother for models, I expected to be both a professional woman and a wife and mother."

In 1917, when Margaret was 15, she seemed well on her way to becoming "a minister's wife with six children." That Christmas she became engaged to Luther Cressman, four years her senior, whom she had met the summer before. As she described her fiancé in her autobiography, "He had an engaging grin and a wry sense of humor, yet he took life seriously and, like my mother, was willing to see life whole." Cressman had planned to become a Lutheran minister; Mead convinced him to switch to the Episcopal church, in which she had been baptized.

That summer was a hard one for Margaret Mead. She had not yet broken the news of her engagement to her family, fearing they would insist she was too young to marry. World War I had been raging since 1914, and Cressman was in officer's training camp, preparing to depart for the European battlefront. (Fortunately, the war ended in 1918, before he was transferred to active duty in Europe.) "My main occupation was being a wartime homemaker on the farm," Mead remarked of this period, in her autobiography. "Twice a week in the afternoons I went to roll bandages at the local Red Cross. . . . In the evenings I wrote my long letters to Luther, filled with poetry."

In the fall of 1918 the Meads moved again, this time to the Pennsylvania town of New Hope. Although she had already graduated from high school, Margaret signed on for classes at the Holmquist School, a private institution in a famous artists' colony. There she studied French so that she could satisfy the language requirement for entrance to her chosen college, Welle-

Margaret launched her college career in 1919. She had planned to attend Wellesley, but her family's financial troubles sent her to DePauw University instead.

sley, where her mother had gone as an undergraduate.

But her carefully laid plans ran aground the following spring, when Edward Mead suffered heavy financial losses in a business venture. He announced that he could no longer afford to send his daughter to college. Emily Mead came to the rescue with a proposal that changed her husband's mind about Margaret's education. She suggested that Margaret attend DePauw University. This was Edward Mead's alma mater, and the idea, Mead said, "captured his interest."

By the summer of 1919, young Margaret Mead's future seemed to be taking shape. "I was 17," she later remarked of this period, "I was engaged to be married. But above all else I was eager to enter the academic world for which all my life had prepared me."

Mead's unusual upbringing complicated her transition to college life. Her eccentricities—a source of pride during her youth—branded her an outsider at DePauw.

THREE

Ash Can Cat

Margaret Mead arrived at DePauw University in the fall of 1919 with high hopes. As she later described her feelings, she looked forward to meeting her fellow students, with whom she longed to "stay up all night talking about things that mattered." Above all, she saw college as a place "where one would find out what one could do in life."

But Mead's dreams were not realized when she arrived at DePauw's Indiana campus. Instead, as she wrote in her autobiography, she was "confronted by the snobbery and cruelty of the sorority system at its worst."

Student social life at DePauw revolved almost entirely around Greek-letter fraternities and sororities, campus organizations that take their names from the Greek alphabet. These groups held parties, dances, and other social events where college students met and got to know one another. Most incoming freshmen received invitations to pledge (apply for membership in) one or more sororities or fraternities. At DePauw, Mead soon discovered, those not invited to pledge, or those invited but turned down for membership, were treated as social outcasts.

Mead received an invitation to the Kappa sorority's rush party, an event at which the group's current members looked over new pledges before deciding, on the basis of clothing and social skills, whom they would accept for membership and whom they would reject. Mead arrived proudly decked out

DePauw student Katharine Rothenberger became a lifelong friend of Mead's. The only Jewish person on campus, Rothenberger was ostracized from mainstream social life.

in an evening dress of her own design, made for her by a seamstress back home. Apparently, no one at the midwestern campus had ever seen anything quite like it. To Mead's surprise, all the sorority sisters, including the woman who had invited her to the party, shunned her. Her clothing, her keen interest in academics, and her eastern accent had all branded her an outsider at DePauw.

Being "different" was something that Mead had sometimes been proud of in her youth; at DePauw she was ostracized for it. No one belonging to a sorority or fraternity would talk to her. With outrage undiminished by the passage of 50 years, Mead recalled in her autobiography: "I was confronted for the first time in my life with being thoroughly unacceptable to almost everyone and on grounds [originality of dress, thought, and expression] in which I had previously been taught to take pride."

Mead's bruised feelings healed gradually, and she managed to make a few friends. "There were five of us oddballs and we formed a little band we called 'The Minority,'" explained Katharine Rothenberger, with whom Mead forged a lifelong friendship. In sharp contrast to the conformity demanded in the Greek-letter societies, The Minority was a diverse group that included a black, a Catholic, and the only Jew on campus. In this group Mead was appreciated for her intelligence and warmth. Rothenberger was one of the first to notice that in Mead "there was a lot there that other people weren't seeing."

In time Mead's fellow students began to appreciate her unique qualities. With her energy and enthusiasm, she was hard to ignore. She wrote and directed a pageant performed by the entire female student body, joined the English honor society Tusitala (which was, interestingly, the Samoan name given to Robert Louis Stevenson), and worked on the campaign that made Rothenberger DePauw's first female student-body president. Mead also worked hard in her classes, which she found less disappointing than the college's social life.

At the end of her freshman year, Mead knew that she would receive invitations from sororities as a sophomore, but by then she had no intention of returning to DePauw. She was tired of being a grudgingly accepted outsider and longed for an environment that was more stimulating. Barnard College seemed like an exciting alternative to DePauw.

Mead found Barnard College (pictured), on Manhattan's Upper West Side, an attractive alternative to DePauw. She transferred there during her sophomore year.

Barnard attracted her in part because it was an all-female college, and Mead's recent experiences had convinced her that bright young women paid a high price for outshining men in class. Mead noticed that women were often considered unfeminine or unattractive simply because they were intellectually able. Some of her peers "played dumb" for the sake of popularity, but Mead would have none of that. At Barnard, she felt she could study without feeling self-conscious about her intelligence.

Other factors also played a role in her decision. Mead was more than ready to exchange the quiet fields of Indiana for the bustling streets of New York City, where Barnard is located. As she would express her feelings years later, a city was "a place where one need never be bored, where there is always the possibility of a new encounter that may change one's life . . . where the shortest walk can be an experience of surprises and delight." New York was also the city where Luther Cressman was attending school.

In the autumn of 1920, Mead arrived at Barnard College, which was associated with Columbia University. Here, at last, she hoped to find the intellectual challenges and friendships she had hoped for all her life.

She moved into a college-owned apartment on West 116th Street with several other Barnard women. The members of this informal group called themselves the Ash Can Cats. Their name came from a remark made about them by a favorite professor, Minor W. Latham. "You girls who sit up all night readin' poetry," the southern-born drama professor once said, "come to class lookin' like ash can cats!"

The Ash Can Cats, many of whom were to maintain lasting friendships, did stay up all night reading and having intellectual arguments, but they also had a keen sense of fun. They were in part a product of their time, the Roaring Twenties, an era marked by youthful frivolity and the abandonment of tradition. Unwilling to remove her eyeglasses in deference to fashion, Mead was by no means one of the breezy flappers of the period. But she did indulge in a bit of rebellion by bobbing her hair in the short style that came to symbolize the carefree attitude of these young women.

The relatively unfettered existence enjoyed by Mead and her friends in fact reflected serious changes taking place in the lives of women. In 1920 the Nineteenth Amendment to the Constitution had finally given women the right to vote, and Mead and her peers were coming of age at a time when women's horizons seemed to be expanding. Looking back to her college days in *Blackberry Winter*, Mead noted that she and her schoolmates "belonged to a generation of young women who felt extraordinarily free—free from the demand to marry unless we chose to do so, free to postpone marriage while we did other things, free from the need to bargain and hedge that had restricted women of earlier generations."

Partially because of these new attitudes and partially because her family had long ignored societal restrictions on women, Mead felt free to pursue whatever interested her. She engaged in an array of political activities, advocating progressive causes and even joining picket lines to show solidarity with workers striking for improved wages and job conditions. At Barnard she edited the school newspaper and signed on for many student activities. Mead's energy was apparent to all who knew her. "She gave off sparks," remarked one of her classmates.

As Mead engaged in these varied pursuits, she began to consider her future. She had begun college intending to become a writer, and she had continued to major in English after she transferred to Barnard. But she soon began to wonder if literature was her true vocation. She could not help but compare herself to her fellow Ash Can Cat Léonie Adams, a gifted poet who was making a name for herself while still in college. Mead felt that she was not nearly as talented as her friend or as committed to literature. She began to consider other fields.

Mead sits for a portrait with two fellow Ash Can Cats. The lively group of college women shared an Upper West Side apartment until Mead married.

Labor protesters stage a demonstration at the Department of Civil Works in New York City. Mead became deeply involved in the fight for fair working conditions during her years at Barnard.

Though continuing with her major in English, Mead decided to take a second major, in psychology. "I wanted to make a contribution," she wrote in her autobiography. "It seemed to me then—as it still does—that science is an activity in which there is room for many degrees, as well as many kinds, of giftedness. It is an activity in which any individual, by finding his own level, can make a true contribution."

An important crossroads came when Mead had to choose between two courses during her senior year. One was in philosophy, the other in anthropology. "I chose anthropology," she related matter-of-factly in *Blackberry Winter*. Her decision, of course, would have dramatic repercussions both in her own life and in the emerging field of anthropology.

The course Mead took was given by Franz Boas, a towering figure in the anthropological community. Nicknamed "Papa Franz" by his students, Boas had left his native Germany in 1883 at the age of 25. After a lengthy stay in the Arctic, where he had gone to study Eskimos, he immigrated to the United States. He then began teaching, first at Clark University in Massachusetts and then at Columbia. In addition to his academic duties, Boas made periodic field trips to study the native peoples of the Pacific Northwest and served as curator at the American Museum of Natural History from 1896 to 1905.

When Mead began studying with Boas, she found her new professor "somewhat frightening." She later described him as a colorful figure, "with his great head and slight, frail body, his face scarred from an old duel." Soon, however, she saw beyond his odd appearance and brusque manner and discovered a brilliant, probing mind. "It wasn't until I got to Franz Boas," Mead later wrote, "that I really had a teacher who elicited my total respect, so that I felt he could give me the ground under my feet."

Boas roused Mead's interest in anthropology, which had not become a distinct field until the end of the 19th century. When Mead began studying the discipline, few scholars had attempted systematic surveys of various cultures. Indeed, Boas was the only full-time faculty member in Columbia University's anthropology department.

The main thrust of Boas's teaching was a forceful refutation of the theory of racial determinism, a concept popular at the time. Racial determinists held that people's intellectual capabilities were linked to their racial origins. This doctrine was frequently used to justify exploiting the people and resources of one culture (often nonwhite) by another (usually white). Boas passionately opposed racial determinism. "A close connection between race and personality," Boas maintained, "has never been established."

Franz Boas also believed that men and women could better understand their own culture if they knew more about other societies. Anthropological data, he felt, could help wipe out harmful prejudices while reinforcing those values that are truly positive and beneficial. But it was crucial, Boas cautioned, for anthropologists to gather this information as soon as possible. Improved transportation and communication, coupled with the tendency of certain cultures to dominate others, were destroying many societies. It was up to anthropologists to mine the world's cultural wealth before it was lost forever.

Mead, who had been raised to consider all races equal and all cultures comparable, was receptive to Boas's theories. Fascinated, she decided to take every course he taught, even though most were graduate-level

Ruth Fulton Benedict became Mead's lifelong friend. A teaching assistant to Franz Boas, Benedict brought anthropology lectures to life for many students.

courses and she was still an undergraduate. Impressed by Mead's enthusiasm and intelligence, Boas allowed her to enroll.

Although deeply immersed in Boas's teachings, Mead had only limited personal contact with him. This was not true of her relationship with anthropologist Ruth Fulton Benedict, then Boas's teaching assistant, who became both mentor and friend to Mead. In her autobiography, Mead described Benedict as a shy woman who always wore the same dress. "She spoke so hesitatingly," she recalled of her teacher, "that many students were put off by her manner." Mead, however, found that Benedict's comments brought Boas's formal lectures to life. She also discovered that Benedict's intense commitment to anthropology was contagious.

By the spring of her senior year, Mead was weighing the possibility of pursuing graduate study in anthropology, though she had already begun her master's thesis in psychology. Her course finally became clear when she lunched with Benedict one day. "Professor Boas and I," Benedict told her, "have nothing to offer but an opportunity to do work that matters." Benedict's simple statement stirred Mead's idealism. "That settled it for me," Mead wrote in *Blackberry Winter*. "Anthropology had to be done *now*. Other things could wait."

Mead's personal life was also taking shape during this period. Months after her June 1923 graduation from Barnard, she married Luther Cressman, who had

Margaret Mead and Luther Cressman married in 1923 after a lengthy engagement. But as their professional lives began to blossom, the couple found they had little in common.

now been her fiancé for six years. Their courtship had been an unconventional one. Though Cressman had been in downtown New York studying at the General Theological Seminary during Mead's Barnard years, they had seen each other only once or twice a week.

The arrangement had suited Mead, who was fond of Cressman but hardly passionate. "If you had a man," according to the ever-practical Mead, "you weren't continually thinking about them." She saw to it that her relationship with Cressman left her time for other things, including schoolwork, social causes, and "deep and creative friendships with women." Her marriage would be the same way: Mead refused to allow it to dominate her life at the expense of other concerns. She decided to keep her own name, she said, in order to act on her mother's belief "that women should keep their own identity and not be submerged."

Newly married, Cressman and Mead settled into a hectic but exciting life. Their tiny Manhattan apartment became a favorite gathering spot for Mead's many friends. Hardly a week passed without one of her or Cressman's acquaintances sleeping on the couch. Mead embarked on graduate work in anthropology and completed her master's thesis in psychology. To help make ends meet, she also worked at several jobs. These included a teaching assistant's position in Barnard's economics and sociology departments and a stint as an editorial assistant for the *Journal of the American Statistical Association*.

At the end of the summer of 1924, Mead attended a meeting of the British Association for the Advancement of Science. The conference had a great influence on her. There, surrounded by working anthropologists abuzz with reports of their latest research, Mead's commitment to her chosen career grew and crystallized. By the time she returned to New York, she was sure that she wanted to do fieldwork of her own as soon as she received her Ph.D. in the spring of 1925.

Cressman and Mead discussed the possibility of going to the field together, but Mead did not think her husband possessed the training or skills that would make him a useful field partner. Cressman, who was doing graduate work in sociology and serving as a part-time pastor at a small Brooklyn church, made a counterproposal. The following year he would get a fellowship to study in Europe; Mead could go her own way to pursue her field research.

Winning her husband's cooperation in her plans for the upcoming year was the easy part for Mead. She then had to cope with Professor Boas, who had very strong opinions on her choice of a field and the anthropological issues she would study there. Mead wanted to examine cultural change in Polynesia; he wanted her to study adolescence among Native Americans.

Boas had reasons for closely supervising his students' fieldwork. Limited funding was available for anthropological research, and there were few people to send into the field. In 1924 four students made up the entire graduate anthropology department at Columbia University, and no more than another handful were studying at other universities. Boas had to decide where best to place each field-worker so that all their efforts would be integrated and neither funds nor research would be wasted.

Mead understood Boas's concerns, yet she was adamant about her choice of location. She had already learned a great deal about Polynesia during her graduate studies and hoped to enhance her knowledge through fieldwork. Finally, Boas gave in to his stubborn protégée, but he insisted that she avoid any islands that were too remote or dangerous. She must, he said, choose an island that was visited regularly by ships, a restriction Mead was willing to accept. In this way she hit upon the idea of traveling to American Samoa, a group of islands in the South Pacific 9,000 miles from the United States. Samoa satisfied Boas's safety concerns because it was a U.S. Navy outpost and American boats called there every three weeks.

Mead won the opportunity to travel to the field of her choice, but Boas convinced her to study adolescence, not cultural change, as she had originally planned. He hoped that her research would help confirm the theory that emotional upheavals experienced by teenagers had cultural rather than biological origins. If Mead could prove the theory, her evidence would support his larger goal: refuting the racial determinists' claim that human character is fixed by race and ancestry.

After the initial details were worked out, Mead's plan took shape rapidly. Edward Mead reluctantly agreed to pay his intrepid daughter's traveling expenses. Boas endorsed her application for a National Research Council fellowship that would partially fund her study. He also defended Mead's choice of field site when others questioned it.

Margaret Mead's final preparations for her Samoan journey were relatively

Mead relaxes with other Barnard students. Although their fields of study led them in different directions, Mead and many of her college friends remained close throughout their lives.

Traditional structures housed the local parliament on Tau island when Mead first visited there. Mead chose the island for its convenience but found it perfect for her research as well.

simple. It took her only a few days to gather some light cotton dresses, an extra pair of glasses, a camera, pencils, and notebooks. Once she got the immunization shots required of travelers to the tropics, she was ready to go. Mead remarked in the late 1970s that modern preparations for fieldwork "take many months and involve not some 20 objects, but, more likely, 2,000." Still, she added, "in spite of all the differences," one thing has not changed. The air of excitement and anticipation surrounding "the last few days before a field trip remains very much the same."

When Margaret Mead arrived in Samoa to begin her fieldwork, she had no idea that she would change the shape of anthropology for future researchers.

FOUR

Fieldwork and Fame

In the summer of 1925, Margaret Mead departed for American Samoa, and Luther Cressman left for Great Britain. The difference in destinations underscored deeper differences between the couple, a fact Mead may not have acknowledged yet but which Cressman had. He arrived in England, he later wrote, "deeply troubled" about his marriage and his future. He and Mead had been growing apart, and their long separation would only contribute to their estrangement. Though they would not divorce until 1928, the marriage was effectively over when Mead set sail for Samoa, leaving behind her student years and the man she later called her "student husband."

Mead spent nine months in Samoa, working tirelessly to compile informa- tion on the villagers of Tau island, particularly the adolescent girls. Her research invigorated and challenged her, but as her time in the field drew to a close, she began to worry. "I had to invent every method I used," she wrote in *Blackberry Winter*, "and I had no way of knowing whether what I had done was good or not."

Despite her doubts, Mead's fieldwork on Tau island would yield fascinating results. Although it had been selected primarily for safety and convenience, Samoa proved to be an excellent scien- tific choice. The information Mead gathered there did much to bolster Boas's theories that culture had a strong influence on individual person- ality. From no other Polynesian cul- ture, Mead noted, would she have

Mead sits atop a Samoan canoe on Tau island. The anthropologist adopted traditional Samoan dress in order to show respect for the island's inhabitants.

gleaned results that so completely challenged the prevalent Western notion that adolescent turmoil was entirely a consequence of biology and was therefore inevitable.

Mead discussed her findings in *Coming of Age in Samoa*. On the Samoan island of Tau, she wrote, she found a people whose morality was less rigid and judgmental than that of Western cultures. These relaxed attitudes affected Samoa's teenagers. Instead of structured and closely supervised dating rituals, for instance, Mead found that adolescent social life was relaxed and easygoing. She wrote of freeform dances in which the participants expressed their feelings and personalities and of trysts between young people under the palm trees on balmy moonlit nights.

In *Coming of Age in Samoa*, Mead observed that the adolescence of Samoan girls was "freer and easier and less complicated" than that of their Western counterparts. With few exceptions, Mead wrote, "adolescence represented no period of crisis or stress, but was instead an orderly developing of a set of slowly maturing interests and activities. The girls' minds were perplexed by no conflicts, troubled by no philosophical queries, beset by no remote ambitions."

Mead suggested that the key reason Samoan girls made a more peaceful transition to adulthood than their Western counterparts was a difference in upbringing. In Samoa, children were exposed to natural life processes every day and thus were prepared for adult life. In Western cultures, however, parents shielded their children from knowledge of sex, childbirth, and death for as long as possible. As a result, Western children often developed fears and misconceptions that surfaced as confusion and rebellion when they entered adolescence.

In Mead's judgment, however, young Samoans paid a price for their smooth transition to adulthood: Compared to Western teenagers, she wrote, they seemed to have "less intensity, less individuality, less involvement with life." Western youths, it seemed, often had more defined, passionate personalities, perhaps because they had to struggle against societal restrictions in order to carve out their niche in the social order.

In *Coming of Age in Samoa*, Mead questioned the value of traditional European and American family life and education. She noted that Western children's experiences were too often limited to their immediate families. Mead felt that youngsters would be better challenged and stimulated by more exposure to the "larger family community, in which there are several adult men and women." As her parents and grandmother had done, Mead also rejected regimented schooling. "Children must be taught how to think," Mead maintained, "not what to think."

The publication of *Coming of Age in Samoa* created a stir that extended far beyond the anthropological community. Mead's vivid, straightforward writing style appealed to many readers, and her book introduced millions to the field of anthropology. Mead's conclusions stunned much of her wide audience. Some were shocked by Mead's nonjudgmental descriptions of a society that condoned premarital affairs and did not consider marriage a sacred bond. And many who considered the rebellion and emotional upheavals of teenagers to be the natural consequence of biology were forced to reconsider their convictions. As her ideas were debated, the name of Margaret Mead, a quiet intellectual who had started a storm, became a household word.

Not only was Mead's professional life forever changed by her Samoan trip, but her romantic life was also

Children gather around Mead and Reo Fortune in Peri village on the island of Manus in Papua New Guinea. The couple married en route to the island for fieldwork.

affected. On the Australia-to-France leg of her voyage home from Polynesia, she had met an intriguing man named Reo Fortune. The handsome 24-year-old New Zealander had been on his way to Cambridge University in England to study psychology. According to Mead, the two talked nonstop during their seven-week sea journey aboard the S.S. *Chitral*—she about her work in the field, he about his just completed master's thesis on dreams. They were, in fact, so deep in conversation when the ship docked in France that Mead and Fortune were the last passengers to disembark. Luther Cressman had to wait on the dock, wondering what had happened to his wife.

Although Mead suspected that she might have more in common with Fortune than with Cressman, she wanted to give her marriage a second chance. She returned to New York, where she and Cressman moved into an apartment on Manhattan's Upper West Side. Her husband had left the ministry and was teaching at City College. Mead, for her part, taught some classes at Columbia and worked on completing the manuscript that would become *Coming of Age in Samoa*.

In the fall of 1926, Mead started a job as an assistant curator at the American Museum of Natural History, a vast institution packed with everything from dinosaur bones to Eskimo kayaks. Her job required her to assess and acquire objects for the museum, work for which she was well suited. She enjoyed her office there, a remote attic room in a high tower. It became a haven where she could think, write, and research. "I decided within a few months," she recalled in *Blackberry Winter*, "that I was going to stay at the Museum all my life."

But other aspects of Mead's life remained unsettled. Her marriage was on shaky ground, and she continued to correspond with Reo Fortune in England. In the summer of 1927, Mead and Fortune vacationed together in Germany. During this trip she made up her mind to leave Cressman. When she returned to New York that fall, it was to an apartment of her own.

Fortune, who had decided to give up psychology for anthropology, left England in late 1927 for his first field trip. He had received funding to study sorcery and religion in New Guinea for two years. Mead planned to join him once she was divorced from Cressman. Fortune decided to extend his work on primitive religions to the Admiralty Islands north of New Guinea; Mead wanted to study children there.

Securing funding and preparing for one person's field trip were complex enough. Arranging for two anthropologists to end up in the same place at the same time was as complicated, Mead said, "as the storied encounters of separated lovers." Nevertheless, she managed it. Backed by another grant from the National Research Council, which had funded her work in Samoa, Mead sailed for New Guinea in the fall of 1928. Fortune met her in New Zealand, where they were married on October 8.

Mead and Fortune chose as their subjects the inhabitants of Manus, one of the Admiralty Islands north of New Guinea. The Manus were a fishing people who lived in houses perched on stilts in the lagoons between the reefs and the shoreline. Mead described Peri, the village they settled in, as a "primitive Venice" in which "all life is conducted by means of canoes."

The difficulties of beginning their field assignments were complicated for Mead and Fortune by the necessity of learning not one but two new languages. The men of Manus, most of whom had some experience working at mines or plantations owned by white settlers, usually spoke Pidgin English. This blend of local dialect and English was also called talk-boy. But the

women, who seldom left their villages, spoke very little Pidgin. Accordingly, Mead and Fortune had to learn two new languages: Pidgin English and the Manus dialect spoken in Peri.

Neither Mead nor Fortune found their subjects congenial. The anthropologists considered the inhabitants of Manus exceptionally materialistic because their entire lives centered around economic exchange and the acquisition of wealth. When a Manus man speaks of his wife, Mead wrote in *Growing Up in New Guinea*, "he mentions the size of the betrothal payment which was made for her. When he speaks of his sister, he says, 'I give her sago and she gives me beadwork'; when he angers

Distinctive stilt houses stand in the waters of Peri village. Mead called the village a "primitive Venice."

Mead's study of childhood in Peri challenged many established theories about the development of behavior patterns. She concluded that adults' values influence children's attitudes.

the spirit of a neighbor's house he atones in pigs and oil or boxes and axes. The whole of his life, his most intimate relations to people, his conception of places . . . all fall under the head of 'kawas,' or exchange.''

The Manus were also a puritanical people who believed that evil acts were punished by a vigilant corps of domineering ghosts and spirits. People who violated taboos or failed to satisfy financial obligations could be dealt with severely by these supernatural beings.

Whenever someone got sick or lost or hurt, it was thought that the spirits were taking their revenge.

Because of such beliefs, the Manus resisted Mead and Fortune's attempts to administer Western medicine to ailing villagers. Early in their stay a child suffered a fall that knocked him unconscious. When the anthropologists tried to help, they were rebuffed and told that the youngster's fate was in the hands of the spirits. Desperate, Mead and Fortune broke open a bottle of ammonia and waved it under the boy's nose. When he revived instantly, the impressed natives let Fortune treat the child's wounds, which turned out to be minor. After this incident the anthropologists had less difficulty ministering to the Peri villagers. They were able to help several sick natives, including some suffering from malaria, a tropical fever that often afflicted Mead herself.

But even repeated displays of the powers of Western medicine did little to shake local superstitions, as Mead would discover when she caught a bad cold. Kilipak, the anthropologist's 13-year-old cook, came down with a fever at the same time. A Manus delegation came to Mead and Fortune's house and announced that they had learned, by way of a séance, that a spirit named Sori was making both Mead and Kilipak sick. Neither would recover, they warned, until Mead and Fortune moved into the new home that had been built for them—a move Mead had postponed because of her cold. In the next two days, two more of their houseboys came down with a fever. The villagers grew insistent, and Mead and Fortune were forced to move at an hour's notice to appease the angry spirit of Sori.

Mead gathered data on Manus culture as a whole, but she paid special attention to the children, her primary subjects. In order to understand how they saw the world around them, she asked the youngsters to draw pictures for her. By the time she left Manus she had collected 35,000 children's drawings. She also studied the youths' daily life. Unlike the young of many other cultures, Manus children had no duties or responsibilities; they were free simply to play. Their games were not just for amusement, however. As Manus children paddled about the lagoons in miniature canoes, fished, and dragged for minnows using pieces of bark as makeshift nets, they mastered skills that would be important when they became adults.

But once they became adolescents, Mead found, "the generous, gay, cooperative Manus children turned into grasping, competitive Manus adults." As soon as they reached maturity, the Peri villagers were expected to acquire enough goods to participate in the economic exchanges that formed the main activity of adult life. This exchange system put the villagers in constant competition with one another.

Comparing the youngsters of Peri village to their elders, Mead reached a startling conclusion. She theorized that children could be given years of freedom that emphasized values different from their parents but that these attitudes would not necessarily last into adult life. "It was no use permitting children to develop different values from those of their society," Mead wrote. "You cannot alter a society by giving its children of school age new behavior patterns to which the adult society gives no scope."

Mead's idea would make waves within the scientific and educational community, because it implied that the impact of new influences on children was limited by the attitudes of adults. Although some hoped that fu-

54

ture generations could be freed from prejudice and other undesirable traits through progressive education alone, Mead maintained that such a strategy would not work. In order to improve society, she insisted, parents and educators should focus not only on schooling children but also on changing their own values. Only this dual approach, she wrote, would accomplish "the vital matter of developing individuals, who as adults, can gradually mould our old patterns into new and richer forms."

After six months in the field, Mead and Fortune left Manus, arriving in New York in September 1929. Mead returned to her post at the American Museum of Natural History, and Fortune won a fellowship at Columbia University. Their relationship, which had thrived in the tropics, grew rocky in the United States. While they were away, *Coming of Age in Samoa* had become a best-seller, and Mead was now something of a celebrity. On the other hand, Fortune was relatively unknown, even within the academic community.

In addition, money was tight. As scholars, neither Mead nor Fortune made very much money. The stock market crashed in October, ushering in the Great Depression, and funds became even scarcer. The Museum of Natural History announced it was reducing staff salaries, including Mead's, which had only been $2,500 a year to start with. But *Coming of Age in Samoa* was still selling well, and she had been careful with the royalties she had already earned. Taking her father's

Although Mead concentrated on the children of Peri, she spent a great deal of time studying the adults of Manus island. She noted that their culture was based entirely on exchange.

55

advice, Mead had transferred her nest egg to a local Pennsylvania bank that escaped the collapse many other banks had suffered. She was glad she had not risked her savings, which would eventually be used to fund future fieldwork.

That winter and spring Mead and Fortune transformed the notes from their Manus field trip into books. Mead worked tirelessly, and her husband fol-lowed her example. In the evenings they read aloud what each had written that day. Mead was an appreciative audience for Fortune's work. She valued her husband's scholarship and his intellect, though she was also a sharp critic when she felt criticism was appropriate. "If we are to have a world in which women work beside men," Mead said, "women must learn to give

Mead displays masks collected in New Guinea. In 1929 she returned to the United States to transform her fieldwork into a book, Growing Up in New Guinea.

up pandering to male sensitivities."

During this period Mead penned *Growing Up in New Guinea*, published in 1930; Fortune wrote the final version of *Sorcerers of Dobu* and began *Manus Religion*. Both of Fortune's books would receive good scholarly reviews, but neither would earn him the fame or popularity that already belonged to his wife.

Mead's reputation was bolstered by the publication of her second book. Although *Growing Up in New Guinea* generated neither the sales nor the controversy of her first published work, it was a critical and commercial success. *Growing Up in New Guinea* not only vividly described a culture but also pointed out the strong similarities between Western men and women and their supposedly "primitive" counterparts.

In the spring of 1930, Dr. Clark Wissler, chairman of the anthropology department of the Museum of Natural History, approached Mead with a pro- posal. The museum had received money to fund a brief field study of Native American women, and Wissler asked Mead to undertake it. More in- terested in studying isolated cultures in far-off places, Mead was not partic- ularly pleased with the assignment.

She began to reconsider her position after Ruth Benedict promised that if Mead would go to the Omaha Indian reservation in Nebraska, funds could be located for Fortune to go along in order to resolve some unanswered questions about tribal religious prac- tices. Furthermore, as biographer Jane Howard pointed out in *Margaret Mead: A Life*, "the Omaha reservation would be as good a place as any for Mead to deepen the niche she had already carved out for herself as an interviewer of women, whom most previous an- thropologists had belittled if not over- looked." The opportunity seemed too good to pass up. In the summer of 1930, Mead and Fortune headed west to em- bark on their second field trip together.

During her years in the field, Margaret Mead collected thousands of artifacts. Many of them are exhibited in the Hall of Oceanic Peoples at New York's American Museum of Natural History.

FIVE

"Sex and Temperament"

Mead and Fortune's 1930 fieldwork with the Omaha Indians proved disappointing. Many things discouraged them: the fierce heat of the Nebraska summer, the scholarly difficulties both anthropologists faced in carrying out their research, and the state of the culture they had come to study. In her book *Letters from the Field*, Mead described the trip as "three strenuous, grueling months" spent "watching the sorrows of a fading culture." One of her goals as an anthropologist was to document non-Western societies before they were completely assimilated into Western culture. In the case of the Omaha, it seemed that she had arrived too late.

Many traditional Omaha beliefs and ceremonies had begun to change in the early 19th century. This cultural reorganization was due in part to the disappearance of the great herds of buffalo that had once roamed the plains and provided the basis of the Omaha's economy. Another factor was the U.S. government's overregulation of Indian affairs. This affected many areas of Omaha life, most notably education. Students were taken from the reservation and educated, Mead observed, by "federal employees who knew little, and usually cared less, about their pupils and the cultures from which they came." The end result, Mead believed, was that young people were increasingly alienated from their traditional culture.

This disintegration of values made itself felt in many ways. "Drunkenness was rife," Mead commented in *Blackberry Winter*. "Broken homes, neglected children, and general social disorganization were evident everywhere." Although Mead found that "there was very little out of the past

59

that was recognizable" in Omaha culture, she and Fortune gathered all the information they could. They documented the traditional dress, dance, ceremony, and religious beliefs of the Omaha. When they returned to New York, Mead and Fortune both published their findings, she in *The Changing Culture of an Indian Tribe*; Fortune in *Omaha Secret Societies*.

The Omaha behind them, Mead and Fortune made plans to leave for the field. They would fund their excursion with the $5,000 nest egg from Mead's book royalties and with matching funds from Columbia University and the Museum of Natural History. In December 1931 the two anthropologists arrived in New Guinea to begin their second field trip there.

They had come to study the Abelam, a people who lived about a two-day walk inland from the Pacific island's northeast coast and over the Torricelli mountains. But the 150 carriers Fortune recruited to carry 6 months' worth of supplies across the mountains abruptly abandoned their jobs, leaving the anthropologists stranded in the mountaintop village of Alitoa. With far too much equipment to manage on their own, Mead and Fortune had no choice but to remain in Alitoa. They settled in with the village's inhabitants, a small tribe of approximately 90 people. This group had no name for themselves; the anthropologists later called them the Mountain Arapesh. While a misadventure had forced them to study the Arapesh, the accident would prove fortuitous. Study of the

tribe would eventually shed light on Mead's chosen field topic, the ways in which culture influences sex roles.

Over the next few months Mead learned sex-based divisions of labor among the Arapesh. When questioned about who performed particular jobs, one Arapesh villager told Mead: "Cooking everyday food, bringing firewood and water, weeding and carrying—these are women's work; cooking ceremonial food, carrying pigs and heavy logs, housebuilding, sewing thatch, clearing and fencing, carving, hunting and growing yams—these are men's work; making ornaments and the care of children—these are the work of both men and women."

Men and women also performed different ceremonial roles. In Alitoa, as in many parts of New Guinea, men worshiped a deity known as the tambaran. The tambaran, the patron of the tribe's grown men, was conceived of as a towering giant. Its "voice" was the sound of the male villagers' flutes and whistles. The sight of the tambaran was forbidden to women and children; whenever the men played the ceremonial flutes, the women and children were required to run away from the sound as fast as possible. Following the tambaran's visit, large wreaths of red leaves appeared at the foot of every palm tree. These, the children were told, were the tambaran's ankle bracelets, which had slipped off.

Just as females were excluded from the tambaran cult, Arapesh women had rituals of their own that excluded men. Childbirth and puberty rites were ex-

Mountain Arapesh shop for headdresses at a market in the New Guinea village of Alitoa. Mead and Fortune came to study the Arapesh by a fortuitous accident.

clusively the women's domain, as was the dyeing of grass skirts. "The very sound of men's voices will spoil the dye," Mead wrote, "just as the sound of women's voices will anger the tambaran."

But despite these few differences, Mead discovered that most Arapesh men and women conformed to a single personality type, one that Western societies often defined as feminine. "Both men and women were expected to be succoring and cherishing and equally concerned with the growth of chil-

dren," she later remarked. When marriages were arranged between very young children, small girls were sent as prospective brides to live with their future in-laws until it was time to marry. Their husbands-to-be helped hunt food for them, to "grow" them, as the Arapesh put it. "The whole adventure of living centered around making things grow," Mead observed. "Plants, pigs, and most of all, children."

Mead's findings threw doubt on the prevailing Western idea that personality differences between men and

Arapesh culture proved an excellent choice for Mead's study of sex roles. The similarities between Arapesh men and women cast doubt on the notion that behavioral gender differences are biologically determined.

women were based on biology. "I had found no temperamental differences between the sexes," she said, "either when I studied their cultural beliefs or when I actually observed individuals. The inference was that such differences were purely a matter of culture, and that in those societies in which cultures disregarded them they did not occur."

Fortune's research was in a totally different area, that of language. He and Mead had been able to pick up the Arapesh tongue well enough to converse with the villagers, but he was having difficulty in recording the grammar that governed their complex language. His frustration was fueled by his conviction that the Arapesh were stubborn and uncooperative. Mead disagreed; she found the Arapesh congenial and helpful.

This was not the only area in which the couple differed. Their marriage, which Mead had envisioned as a harmonious working partnership, was growing increasingly troubled. Mead's dissatisfaction was compounded by her isolation. When Fortune journeyed to surrounding villages, Mead, afflicted with a bad ankle that prevented her from traveling, had to stay behind. After a while, each day—or moon, as the Arapesh measured time—began to seem very much like the one before. "I even begin to wonder what the date is," Mead wrote in a letter home.

Mead and Fortune left Alitoa in August 1932. For their next field site they sought a village that was nearby, accessible by water, and relatively protected from the influence of government officials, missionaries, and neighboring tribes. This brought them to Kenakatem, a Sepik River village inhabited by the Mundugumor. This fierce, aggressive people had been headhunters and cannibals until such practices were outlawed by the government three years prior to Mead and Fortune's field trip.

The anthropologists had been advised to lay in a good supply of buttons, because the Mundugumor had a liking for them. This was all the information they had on the tribe until they arrived in Kenakatem. Although Mead would not realize it during her stay, once again their rather haphazard choice of site would prove fortunate for her research on sex roles.

The Mundugumor, Mead wrote in *Blackberry Winter*, "contrasted with the Arapesh in every conceivable way. Fierce, possessive men and women

A Mundugumor woman and her child in Kenakatem, New Guinea. Mead found that the aggressive Mundugumor villagers contrasted sharply with their passive Arapesh neighbors.

were the preferred type; warm and cherishing men and women were culturally disallowed." Though the Mundugumor were supposedly no longer headhunters, Mead and Fortune decided not to allow more than two or three villagers into their house at one time "lest a head so easily taken might prove too tempting."

As Mead studied the Mundugumor, she realized that they were hostile not only to other adults but to their own children. Before a Mundugumor baby was even born, there was much discussion as to whether it would be allowed to survive. If it was of the "wrong" sex (women preferred boys; men, girls), the infant might be thrown into the river to drown. Babies were kept in woven net bags, as Arapesh infants had been. "But whereas the Arapesh net bag is flexible," Mead later noted, "and interposes no barrier between the child and its mother's warm body, the Mundugumor basket is harsh and stiff and opaque." When a Mundugumor baby cried, it was not picked up or fed; instead, whoever happened to be nearby simply scratched on the outside of the carrying basket in a halfhearted attempt to appease the child.

The more Mead learned about the Mundugumor, the more repelled she was. Scientific detachment, she discovered early in her fieldwork, is hard to maintain while living with a people day in, day out. In Kenakatem, Mead was especially upset by the lack of interest tribe members displayed toward the health and happiness of their children.

Just as they had had different reactions to the Arapesh, Mead and Fortune responded in opposite ways to the Mundugumor. Fortune was both appalled and fascinated by his latest subjects; "they struck some note in him that was thoroughly alien to me," Mead recalled. Among a fierce people, Fortune became fierce himself. Though he had nursed Mead gently during her first attack of malaria in Manus, his approach to the recurrent bouts she suffered in Kenakatem was to ignore them.

Mead was exhausted and depressed by the time they left the Mundugumor shortly before Christmas, 1932. Although she felt that she was learning a great deal about differences between cultures, she was making no headway on her original goal, studying gender differences within cultures. For in both the Mundugumor and the Arapesh cultures men and women shared similar character traits, even though these traits differed greatly between the two cultures. Convinced that her study of these two peoples had yielded what appeared to be useless results, Mead was disappointed. "As far as my central problem was concerned," Mead said, "I felt completely stalemated. There would, of course, be plenty of new material, but not on the subject on which I had particularly wanted to work."

Mead and Fortune planned to spend the Christmas holidays at Ambunti, an Australian government station on the Sepik River. On their way they stopped off at Kankanamun, where British anthropologist Gregory Bateson was carrying out his research. Bateson took one look at Mead, noticed her exhaustion, and found her a chair. Mead later remarked that the concern this stranger expressed for her fatigue marked "the first cherishing words I had heard from anyone in all the Mundugumor months."

Mead, Fortune, and Bateson traveled to Ambunti for Christmas. Isolation had made Bateson desperate for conversation; Mead and Fortune, disenchanted with each other, felt the same way. Bateson was tall, youthful, and possessed of "all the assurance of his English background and the intellectual certainty of his Cambridge education." It did not take long, Mead recalled, before she and Bateson had established "a kind of communication" in which Fortune did not participate. This did not bode well for her marriage, for as Mead once remarked of her husband, he was so jealous "he begrudged even the attention I gave to a piece of mending."

Mead and Fortune had enough funds for several additional months of fieldwork, and they consulted with Bateson on their next choice of field site. They decided to study a tribe that lived on Tchambuli Lake, said to be the most beautiful lake in New Guinea. As her writings reveal, Mead shared this assessment of Tchambuli: "On its black polished surface thousands of pink and white lotuses and blue water lilies are spread, and in the early morning white osprey and blue herons stand in the shallows." She and her husband estab-

Mead met fellow anthropologist Gregory Bateson (left) while studying the Mundugumor with Reo Fortune (right). Three years later, she would end her marriage to Fortune and marry Bateson.

lished their camp a few miles from the village of Aibom, where Bateson set up his new research site. Occasional visits and frequent messages passed between the two locations.

In Tchambuli, Mead and Fortune found what they had been seeking—"a place where things were going on." Mead had considered the cultures of

Mead and Fortune found a challenging case study in the village of the Tchambuli people. The villagers spent a great deal of time conducting elaborate ceremonies and rituals.

the Arapesh and the Mundugumor "very thin," but the opposite was true of Tchambuli. There they discovered an elaborate culture dedicated to art and ritual. "It cannot be said that in order to initiate young boys the Tchambuli hold a ceremony," Mead commented, "but rather that in order to hold a ceremony, the Tchambuli initiate young boys."

Another reason Mead found Tchambuli more interesting than their last two field sites was that she was at last able to study a society with strong gender-based differences. Interestingly, she discovered that these roles represented "a genuine reversal of the sex-attitudes of our own culture, with the [Tchambuli] woman the dominant, impersonal managing partner, the man the less responsible and the emotionally dependent person."

Though Tchambuli men were nominally in charge of their households, the women controlled all valuables and managed most of the family's day-to-day business in a practical, evenhanded manner. The men spent their time carving and painting, gossiping, and playing out their rivalries. This pattern started in childhood. "Tchambuli," Mead remarked, "is the only culture in which I have worked in which the small boys were not the most upcoming members of the community, with the most curiosity and the freest expression of intelligence. In Tchambuli it was the girls who were bright and free."

As she analyzed the gender patterns of Tchambuli, all of her fieldwork in New Guinea began to make sense. "Tchambuli," Mead said, "was providing a kind of pattern—in fact, the missing piece—that made possible a new interpretation" of what she and some of her fellow anthropologist had long suspected: that most people become

A Tchambouli man carves a mask. Mead's analysis of gender patterns in Tchambouli society helped her formulate a theory that proposed that roles for men and women were determined culturally rather than biologically.

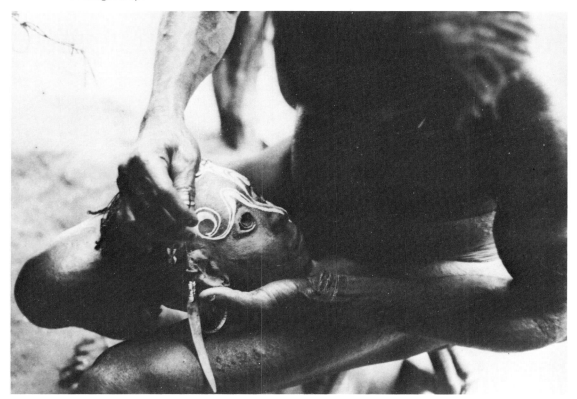

When Mead returned to New York in 1933, her marriage was crumbling, but her work on her most important book—Sex and Temperament in Three Primitive Societies—*was just beginning.*

what their culture expects them to become.

"The Arapesh ideal," she had found, "is the mild, responsive man married to the mild, responsive woman; the Mundugumor ideal is the violent, aggressive man married to the violent, aggressive woman." Tchambuli cul-

ture, on the other hand, "has arbitrarily permitted certain human traits to women, and allotted others, equally arbitrarily, to men." Mead concluded that "the evidence is overwhelmingly in favor of the strength of social conditioning." Both men and women, she had found, developed the personality their society deemed acceptable for their sex. Temperament, in short, was determined by society, not biology. Furthermore, the variations Mead had documented in different cultures supported the position that gender roles were hardly universal. There was no "right" or "wrong" way to be male or female.

Mead found this idea fascinating— not only intellectually but also personally. She herself had often felt that she did not fit in with the image of the ideal American woman of her era, who was a homemaker whose life revolved around a husband and children. "It was exciting," Mead remarked in *Blackberry Winter*, "to strip off the layers of culturally attributed expected behavior and to feel that one knew at last who one was."

Their fieldwork finished, Mead and Fortune cabled Franz Boas that they were coming home with "immensely important" new theoretical points. They had made a tremendous discovery concerning gender and temperament. On a less happy note, Mead and Fortune had concluded that their own temperaments were too much at odds.

When they left New Guinea in the spring of 1933, Gregory Bateson, Reo Fortune, and Margaret Mead went their separate ways. Bateson went home to Cambridge. Fortune continued his anthropological studies in London. Mead returned to New York, to resume work at the American Museum of Natural History and to begin writing what she would consider the most important work of her career, *Sex and Temperament in Three Primitive Societies*.

Margaret Mead made her third trip to New Guinea in 1938. She and her third husband, Gregory Bateson, would use data gathered there to shed light on their study of Balinese culture.

SIX

Bali

Margaret Mead and Reo Fortune were divorced in July 1935. They had not lived together—or even seen each other—since their return from New Guinea two years earlier. Mead had spent those years working at the Museum of Natural History, teaching at Columbia University, lecturing around the country, and finishing *Sex and Temperament*. By this time she had become anthropology's most visible spokesperson. Newspapers and other publications sought her out for interviews, and numerous articles in magazines and journals carried Mead's increasingly familiar byline. "She isn't planning to be the best anthropologist," Ruth Benedict once joked about her longtime friend, "but she *is* planning to be the most famous."

After her divorce, Mead made plans to travel to Bali, an island in Indonesia. Her fourth visit to the South Seas would be the longest and most complex of Mead's many anthropological excursions. The trip also had personal significance: It would be a sort of working honeymoon for Mead and Gregory Bateson, who married in Singapore on March 13, 1936. Since their initial meeting in New Guinea the two anthropologists had kept in touch, and their intense friendship had given way to deeper feelings. Mead hoped that her stay in Bali with her new husband would mark the beginning of the "perfect intellectual and emotional working partnership" she had always wanted.

The couple arrived on the island of Bali a few weeks after their wedding. They planned to gain an overview of Balinese society, paying special attention to the relationship between schizophrenia and culture. Mead wanted to find out whether childhood

71

experiences and societal influences might predispose a person to this severe mental disorder, which robs a person of the ability to act or think in a rational way.

When they arrived in Bali, Mead's first impression was of absolute silence. There were no throngs of people in the villages, no faces peering over the high walls that bordered the roads. No dogs barked, no cooking fires were visible, no children played in front of the houses. Mead and Bateson drove for three hours straight across the island, past rice fields, palm groves, and walled villages. There were no sounds, no signs of life. It was, said Mead, "an experience we will never have again."

Mead and Bateson's arrival had accidentally coincided with the Balinese New Year, a day on which all activity and all noise was forbidden. It was a peaceful and uncharacteristic introduction to a country where, Mead said, "we were never again out of the sound of music." As Mead and Bateson soon discovered, Bali teemed with sound and spectacle: the music of orchestras and

The Balinese village of Bajoeng Gede (pictured) provided Mead with a rich source of data on child rearing. The anthropologist discovered a new use for photography there—the creation of a pictorial record of human life.

operas, flutes and cymbals, drums and gongs; the sounds of people singing; and the dreamy clank of wooden cowbells.

Compared with some of the other places Mead had studied, Bali was an anthropologist's paradise. The country had good roads, which made it easy to travel from one village to another. Its villages, compact and close together, were always crowded with people and activity. And the entire population—over 1 million strong—spoke Balinese, Malay, or both. This pattern contrasted sharply with the New Guinea cultures Mead had studied, where language, much to her frustration, often varied from village to village. In Bali, Mead and Bateson also found a group of Americans and Europeans studying Balinese art and music. Some of these people became the anthropologist's friends; others, collaborators with whom they pooled information.

But what most excited Mead and Bateson was that Balinese culture was packed with the rituals and celebrations that provide anthropologists with insight into the values that define a society. "As one passed along the well-kept roads," Mead said, "one passed from a feast in one temple to a feast in another and met people dressed in glowing colors and carrying offerings. We feasted on riches and found each temple, each theatrical performance . . . more delightful and more intelligible than the last."

For their first two months in Bali, Mead and Bateson concentrated on learning the language and finding a village in which to start their work. They had as their tutor and secretary I Madé Kaler, a young Balinese man who knew five languages, including English. Mead and Bateson opted to learn Balinese rather than Malay, a decision they later regretted because Balinese was much more complicated than Malay. Nonetheless, they eventually mastered the basics of the language.

In May, Mead and Bateson found the village where they wished to settle, a mountain community called Bajoeng Gede. They had a house built and settled down to get to know the 500 village inhabitants and their customs. The choice of site, Mead later noted, would prove another "one of those lucky accidents that have accompanied me all my life." Bajoeng Gede reflected much of the richness of the larger Balinese culture, but the sleepy pace of the mountain village enabled Mead and Bateson to observe and document all important cultural events.

In Bajoeng Gede the anthropologists rapidly learned about Balinese society, sometimes the hard way. On one of their first days there, a local priest named Poepoe paid them a visit to announce that they would have to pay a fine. While strolling around the village, Mead had visited the cemetery. Poepoe informed them that burial grounds were forbidden to women. After some haggling, the couple agreed to pay half the cost of a new cow for the village herd.

This experience caused Mead and Bateson to investigate what else might be forbidden in Bajoeng Gede. They

Balinese women prepare for a ceremony in Bajoeng Gede. The ritual life of the people of Bali has long been the subject of anthropological study.

discovered a long list of taboos. A man with curly hair, or whose wife had curly hair, could not become a village elder, nor could a widower, a great-grandfather, a man with two wives, or a man whose youngest child had married. People could not have mattresses. If one visited a house where there was a newborn baby, one became ceremonially unclean and could not visit any other house for a full day.

While settling in at Bajoeng Gede, racing from religious ceremonies to trance dances to cockfights, Mead and Bateson were also pioneering new fieldwork methods that would change the way anthropologists gathered and used data. Before arriving in Bali, they had decided to use both moving and still photographs to document their research. Bateson had brought along 75 rolls of film to carry them through 2 years.

"One afternoon," Mead recalled, "when we had observed parents and children for an ordinary 45-minute period, we found that Gregory had taken three whole rolls." The couple realized that if they were going to continue taking photographs at such a pace, film processing would require an enormous increase in their work load—and in the amount of money they would need to complete their study. After much discussion, though, they decided they could not pass up the opportunity to use photographs and movies to capture life in Bali. They would eventually take dozens of movies and over 25,000 still photographs. Many of these pictures would appear in their joint book, *Ba-linese Character: A Photographic Analysis*, giving Western readers a glimpse of some of the richness and pageantry of life in Bali. With Bateson behind the camera and Mead taking notes on everything she observed—posture and gesture, paintings and plays, dances and religious rites—the anthropologists missed little.

After a year in Bajoeng Gede, Mead and Bateson moved on to two other Balinese villages, Bangli and Batoean. In these two villages they spent a year rounding out their study of Bali. Although they had originally planned to return home after completing this work, Mead and Bateson now found that they were missing something. "We had, it was true, an unprecedented amount of material," Mead later said. "But the essence of anthropological work was comparison. There was nothing anywhere to compare with what we had." No other culture had ever been the subject of the kind of extensive photographic documentation the couple had done in Bali.

Although Mead and Bateson were exhausted, they felt that they had to remedy this situation right away because of ominous political developments that would soon affect even the remote South Pacific. The news they received from home was two months old, but it was nonetheless clear that the world was fast approaching war. A 1938 letter from Bateson's mother warned that German leader Adolf Hitler was "terribly crazy and altogether amoral." Given the rising tensions in Europe and the Pacific, there was no way of knowing when Mead and Bateson—or anyone else—might be able to return to the field.

The anthropologists traveled back to New Guinea's Sepik River area in March 1938. They gave themselves six months to collect data to compare with the information they had gathered in Bali. Realizing that they would have neither the money, the energy, nor the time to tackle a culture and language entirely new to both of them, they chose to work with the Iatmul people, whom Bateson had studied before.

They settled in Tambunam, a large Iatmul village. A motor-equipped canoe gave the anthropologists access to Tambunam's mile-long waterfront so that they could attend ceremonies and observe day-to-day life around the village. In contrast to the placid residents of Bali, Mead found the Iatmul to be a passionate group, "gay, irresponsible and vigorous, always either laughing or

A father and son perform a ritual dance in a Balinese ceremony. Mead considered the time she spent in Bali to be a model "of what anthropological fieldwork can be like."

screaming with rage. . . . When anyone loses his or her temper, the bystanders stand about, grinning from ear to ear, feeling reassured that this is a world in which people can lose their tempers HARD."

After a series of setbacks in her research, Mead herself lost her temper. She had given up an opportunity to accompany a crocodile hunt in order to witness the birth of a long-overdue baby. The birth had been so near for so long that even the woman's husband scolded his wife for her slowness. The expectant mother had replied that children were born in their own time. Mead—and the expectant parents—waited and waited. The baby was finally born—in its own time—during a fishing trip.

Having missed the birth, Mead consoled herself with the thought that at least she would not miss the baby's first bath, another important Iatmul custom. But she reached the breaking point when she heard that the bath had already taken place. Mead later reported that she and Bateson responded in "proper Iatmul fashion. I smashed a glass and Gregory went and smashed a big Ceram shell on the father's house post. Then we found out it was a false alarm. . . . I was so relieved! I find I don't enjoy displays of anger as much as the Iatmul do."

The Iatmul were also loud and demonstrative in their mourning practices. They were skeptical of those who handled grief in a quieter, more private manner. This attitude was the "one harsh note" Mead found in the culture,

A father plays with his daughter in Bajoeng Gede. The relaxed child-rearing practices of Balinese parents contrasted sharply with those of the Iatmul of New Guinea.

and she witnessed it firsthand. After a two-year-old boy died, his mother did not howl and rant in typical Iatmul fashion. Instead, slow, painful tears fell from her eyes during her son's funeral.

The mother's quiet grief branded her an outcast. She was unmercifully

Mead and Bateson analyzed and compiled vast amounts of data during their stay in Iatmul, New Guinea. They published several books on their joint fieldwork.

scolded, Mead reported, by "a terrible old woman." The child's father was also appalled by his wife's reaction. Mead wrote that he "went away with the next recruiter to work for the white man so that he might not have to stay and watch his wife's lack of feeling." Mead found this episode heartbreaking; she had understood the depth of the woman's sorrow, but the Iatmul had not and had shunned her in her time of need.

After six months with the Iatmul, Mead and Bateson felt they had the material they needed to put their experiences in Bali in perspective. They could contrast the maternal behavior of Balinese women, who borrowed other infants to make their own children jealous, with that of Iatmul women, who took pains to keep their children from feeling jealousy. And they could compare the role that the performing arts played in each culture. Balinese dramas were filled with action and conflict, yet day-to-day life was placid and even. Conversely, the passionate Iatmul, who spent a great deal of time arguing and shouting, used artistic performances to inject calm into their lives.

Mead and Bateson had also paid much attention to gesture and trance in Bali and how these two behavioral patterns might be related to schizophrenia. They found that in addition to the public trance dances that were part of Balinese ceremonial life, individuals frequently went into trances on their own. Mead and Bateson termed this a state of "awayness" and believed it enabled the Balinese to withdraw from stressful situations that otherwise might push them to the breaking point.

Mead considered the work she and her husband had accomplished in Bali the most fruitful and satisfying of her career. "I have tried to replicate the Balinese experience in many different and, on the whole, unsatisfying ways," she said many years later. To her, the trip was a model "of what anthropological fieldwork can be like, even if the model includes the kind of extra intensity in which a lifetime is condensed into a few short years."

Margaret Mead plays with her daughter, Mary Catherine Bateson.
Mead's decision to document her daughter's birth on film was
unconventional at the time, as was her insistence on giving birth
without painkillers.

SEVEN

Culture and Change

After more than two years in the South Seas, Margaret Mead and Gregory Bateson returned to New York in 1939. Soon after their arrival, Mead, who had suffered several miscarriages and been told she would never have children, received startling news: She was pregnant.

Mary Catherine Bateson was born on December 8, 1939, "and looked," said her mother, "very much herself." Bateson and Mead had decided to name their daughter Mary, after one of Bateson's aunts, and Catherine, for Mead's sister who had died in infancy. They called the baby Cathy.

Just as Mead's own birth in a hospital had been unconventional at the time, Cathy's was also unusual. Long before natural childbirth was in vogue, Mead decided to use no painkillers so that she could fully experience her daughter's birth. Even more surprising, she arranged to have the delivery documented on film. Her field experience enabled Mead to adopt this calm approach. In the South Seas she had seen many women give birth without treating it as a traumatic event. Bearing children, Mead believed, was a natural process that should be handled naturally.

Mead also believed that raising children could be compatible with pursuing a career. She had seen mothers in the South Seas going about their daily activities with their babies swaddled against them, and she also had role models closer to home. "My mother and my grandmother," Mead remarked in her autobiography, "had both had children and also used their minds and had careers in the public world."

Accordingly, Mead resumed her professional life several months after Cathy was born. In the spring of 1940

A young American woman welds ammunition magazines for use in World War II. Mead examined American attitudes toward war in her 1942 book, And Keep Your Powder Dry.

she and Bateson selected the 759 photographs that would be included in their book *Balinese Character: A Photographic Analysis.* They also compiled several films, including *Trance and Dance in Bali* and *First Days in the Life of a New Guinea Baby.* In 1940, Mead began writing her next book, a study of contemporary America called *And Keep Your Powder Dry.*

This latest work examined various aspects of modern American life, including ordinary citizens' attitudes toward war. *And Keep Your Powder Dry* was timely because World War II was raging across Europe as Mead wrote. The United States would enter the conflict by the time her book was published. "In writing it," Mead wrote in the preface, "I attempted to use all my experience gained through the study of primitive societies . . . to present the culture and character of my own people in a way they would find meaningful and useful in meeting the harsh realities of war."

In the book Mead also called on Americans to reevaluate their society and to strive for greater equality. She stated that "every social institution which teaches human beings to cringe to those above and step on those below must be replaced by institutions which teach people to look each other straight in the face." *And Keep Your Powder Dry* was a critical and popular success. A reviewer for the Book-of-the-Month Club called it "a stimulating and refreshing exposition of what makes America tick."

In the early 1940s, Mead and Bateson immersed themselves in the war effort. They joined the Committee on National Morale, a group of social scientists who hoped to use their expertise to muster the volunteer effort that was so important during World War II. Mead also felt that anthropologists could help explain the rise of racist leaders such as Adolf Hitler. She charged that Hitler and his followers were endangering the world with a "social virus" of "systematized hatred."

In order to devote herself to war work, she took a leave of absence from her scholarly pursuits at the Museum of Natural History and Columbia University. Commuting between New York and Washington, D.C., she served as executive secretary for the National Research Council's Committee on Food Habits. In this post Mead investigated ways in which people, both in the United States and in war-torn nations overseas, could get the food they needed. Bateson, meanwhile, taught a course in Pidgin English to navy per-

Washington, D.C., hummed with activity during World War II. Mead served as executive secretary for the National Research Council's Committee on Food Habits during this time.

sonnel headed for the Pacific battle-front.

Because their work often took them away from home, Mead and Bateson had to change their living arrangements in order to provide a stable environment for their daughter. They gave up their Manhattan apartment and joined the large Greenwich Village household of some old friends, Larry and Mary Frank. Life at the Franks' Manhattan home exposed Cathy to the kind of family experience Mead had enjoyed as a child, with several generations living together in one household. Larry Frank had five children from two earlier marriages, and an assortment of friends and relatives moved in and out of the house. Mary Catherine Bateson recalled in her 1984 memoir, *With a Daughter's Eye*, that she had grown up "as a member of a flexible and welcoming extended family, full of children of all ages." This unusual and happy household would be home to Cathy and her mother until 1955, when Larry Frank retired and sold the town house.

But while their daughter thrived, Mead and Bateson's marriage disintegrated. Their work during World War II had often kept them apart, and when the conflict ended in 1945, Bateson chose not to return to the marriage or to the kind of work he and Mead had done together. Instead, he focused more on psychology than anthropology. Though Mead had viewed their marriage as a perfect working partnership, Bateson did not. "It was almost a principle of pure energy," he said of the breakup of his relationship with Mead. "I couldn't keep up and she couldn't stop. . . . She could sit down and write 3,000 words by 11 o'clock in the morning, and spend the rest of the day working at the museum."

Mead and Bateson divorced in 1950. It was the only one of her marriages Mead herself did not choose to end. According to friends, Gregory Bateson was the husband Mead had loved, and would miss, the most. "My years as a collaborating wife, trying to combine intensive fieldwork and an intense personal life, came to an end," said Mead of her third divorce. "From that time on I worked not with one other person but with many."

In 1952, Mead planned to return to the field. She had heard that enormous changes had taken place in Manus, New Guinea, where she had worked with Reo Fortune in 1928. She wanted to see—and chronicle—those changes herself. As she told the people of Manus after she arrived there in July 1953, she decided to study them "because of the great speed with which you have changed, and in order to find out more about how people change, so that this knowledge can be used all over the world."

Assisted by 2 young students, Theodore and Lenora Schwartz, Mead set up operations in Peri, the Manus village she had studied 25 years before. The changes she discovered there were enormous. The natives had discarded all the trappings of their old culture. Gone, Mead said, were "the ornaments

. . . the dog's teeth and shell money . . . the arranged marriages, the name taboos, the customs surrounding childbirth, puberty, marriage."

Gone, too, was the old village with its houses set up on stilts like flamingos over the lagoon. The village had been rebuilt on dry land. New houses had been constructed out of the tons of scrap material left behind by the U.S. Army during World War II, when Manus had been an army base.

Some of the changes in Peri were traceable to the natives' formation of a "cargo cult," a form of worship that mushroomed throughout New Guinea and Melanesia following the war. Cargo cults forecasted the messiahlike return of the people's ancestors, who would throw out the white settlers and bestow all the settlers' goods—their "cargo"—on the natives.

Some cargo cults held that followers could receive this cargo only if they destroyed all their present property, uprooted their gardens, and killed their domestic animals. But the Manus villagers had destroyed only burdensome customs. Gone was the system of economic exchange that had forced them to labor constantly, amassing food and possessions to be used as gifts. Gone, too, was the system of penalties that had inhibited relationships between men and women. The cargo cult, in conjunction with exposure to the attitudes and technology of the American soldiers who streamed through New Guinea during the war, had given the Manus a new way of life.

In July 1953, Mead returned to Manus, New Guinea. She hoped to study the changes in traditional culture brought about by the war.

Anthropology student Theodore Schwartz accompanied Mead on her 1953 trip to New Guinea. He and his wife, Leonora, helped record changes that had occurred in Peri during the previous 20 years.

These changes made Peri more interesting to Mead. Though the old village had been picturesque, the anthropologist felt that "the angry voices, the strident drums, the shouting and the turmoil somehow spoiled the lovely sunsets and fair moonlit nights. Now the air is filled . . . with the sound of ukuleles and of children playing singing games."

The changes in Peri were all the more striking to Mead because of their impact on people she had known 25 years earlier. One of these was Manuwai, who had been her 16-year-old houseboy during her 1928 visit. Manuwai, Mead remembered, had seemed fated to grow up to be like his brusque, aggressive father. But she was pleasantly surprised to find that Manuwai, a middle-aged man by the time of her second visit, had mellowed considerably. He invited the anthropologist to his home and proudly introduced her to his wife and mother-in-law. "*You* know what this means," he told Mead. "*You* know that before I could never have spoken to her mother. That I could never have called my wife by name, never have sat down with her or eaten with her." Mead was impressed. In the past, she knew, he would have been expected to display only "shame and aversion" toward these women, no matter what his true feelings were.

Other old friends showed Mead that relations between members of the same sex had also improved under Manus's new order. A villager named Kutan and Kilipak, Mead's former cook, had been close boyhood friends during Mead's first visit; their friendship was still strong decades later. In 1928 she had noted that boyhood friendships never survived the passage into adulthood, when all men became economic rivals. But in 1953 she saw Kutan and Kilipak, both now middle-aged, amiably working side by side. "In the past a man might work so with a younger brother," Mead recalled, "but not with a man of equal strength and worth." Once the Manus's elaborate economic exchanges were eliminated, friendships between adults began to flourish.

Kilipak, Kutan, and Manuwai reminisced with Mead about the Peri of 1928. "When I showed them photographs of their old way of life," she remarked, "grown men of 40 would laugh in an amused, almost tender fashion at pictures of their dead elders wreathed in leaves and dog's teeth, brandishing obsidian-pointed spears." But the young villagers, Mead discovered, "disliked the pictures of a past which they had never known. For them, the old ornaments and flamboyant hairdressing . . . were symbols of pure evil. Their first vivid social experience had been seeing the elders inaugurate the new order by pitching strands of dog's teeth, spears and daggers, ornamented baskets and carved slit gongs into the sea."

Although the people of Manus seemed to embrace wholeheartedly the changes in their culture, Mead had mixed feelings about them. She saw "incipient tragedy" ahead for a people so dependent on the cast-off scraps and equipment of the U.S. Army; a people

Mead returned from Peri with the makings of a book, New Lives for Old, *published in 1960. The work was a comprehensive analysis of cultural change in action.*

who, in giving up the food stockpiling that had fueled their economic exchange system, had also given up storing food for any reason. The villagers of Peri now lived a precarious hand-to-mouth existence. In the event of a natural disaster, such as a flood or a hurricane, they would have no reserves of food to fall back on.

Mead also found it sad that in their eagerness to replace all their old customs with modern ones, the Peri villagers had made certain aspects of their lives more difficult. Once reliant on the angle of the sun to tell time, the villagers now insisted that clocks be used. But as there were only two clocks and one watch in the village, events, Mead said, "were less likely to start on time than when meetings were set by the sun." Furthermore, although the Manus had a taste for modern fabrics and building supplies, they did not have the writing skills or the postal services necessary to send for them. Rising expectations, it seemed, had far outpaced cultural development.

Mead left Peri in December 1953. In *New Lives for Old*, the book she published three years later, Mead described the courage, wisdom, and innocence the Peri villagers displayed as they reshaped their society in "a collective assertion of the dignity of man." She had found "the whole thing fascinating," she said, referring to the changes she had observed in Peri. "Fascinating, a little heartbreaking, but also something that makes one proud of the human race."

Although she retired from active fieldwork after 1953, Margaret Mead continued to make many trips abroad. In 1963 she toured Greece with a group that included author-inventor Buckminster Fuller (in bowtie).

EIGHT

Becoming a Legend

The 1953 trip to Manus was the last in which Margaret Mead did a major share of the fieldwork herself. Though field excursions were luxurious compared to what they had been when she began her career nearly 30 years earlier, they were still difficult, exhausting undertakings. Harsh climates remained harsh; villages once infested with mosquitoes were still infested. It was still difficult to adjust to the customs, food, and languages of unfamiliar cultures. Mead, now well into middle age, was quite willing to literally leave the field to others.

Nevertheless, Mead continued to travel to far-off places. Between the late 1950s and the mid-1970s, she made a number of what she termed "field visits," all of which were relatively brief. These visits were possible because of the growth of air travel: Trips to dis-

tant, once nearly inaccessible places that had taken weeks by ship and on foot now took only hours by plane. Mead's field sojourns were as short as five days and as long as two months. In each case she collaborated with someone else—a student, a colleague, or a photographer.

In 1957, Mead revisited Bali with photographer Ken Heyman, who also visited many other countries and cultures to gather material for a pictorial book, *Family*, which he and Mead compiled together. *Family*, published in 1965, used photographs to illustrate the similar ways that family members related to each other despite great differences in the cultures from which they came.

Another field visit brought Mead back to Peri, Manus, in 1964–65. This third trip to Manus gave her a chance

Mead returned to Bali in 1957 to collect data for a book called Family. *Published in 1965, the book covered the people of Bali, as well as many other societies studied by the anthropologist with photographer Ken Heyman.*

to observe further changes in the village she had first studied in 1928. "I live," Mead wrote upon arriving in Peri in late 1964, "neck deep in the past." Most of the villagers were rushing headlong into the future, but at least one shared her urgency about chronicling the beliefs and practices of bygone days. Pokanau, who had been one of Mead and Reo Fortune's main informants in 1928, was now near 70. He was, Mead said, "very anxious that all he knows be taken down on the tape recorder. He realizes that soon there will be no one who knows the old war songs and the tales of his people's wanderings as they spread out and built one village after another in the wide seas." He wanted this record of the old tales and customs to survive.

Mead faithfully recorded the old man's recollections of the past, just as she chronicled the young Manus's "race towards the future." The villagers now had many opportunities for education. In 1964, 33 Manus men and women were studying in urban New Guinea and Australia; some of them would return to their native island as trained nurses or teachers.

But along with these expanded horizons came prejudices against newly educated Manus women. Though young women were encouraged to pursue their scholarly aspirations, most of the men of Manus still preferred traditional wives, a holdover from the customs of their parents and grandparents. Mead noted that educated Manus women were "treated as damaged goods and no one wants to marry them."

Mead was concerned about the fate of these women—and about the future of the village as a whole. She and the elders of Peri were alarmed that many of the youths who left the island to study never returned. The older people were worried that there would be fewer and fewer young people to care for them, and they were particularly concerned that no one would be there to

build their houses. During Mead's stay, two old men staged "a near-death scene" to dramatize their plight. Their point was heeded, and building began. But Mead knew that if the exodus of Peri's youth continued, one day there would not be enough able-bodied young people left to build houses—or keep the already ailing culture of the Manus alive.

Mead also anticipated that she would see changes in the Iatmul village of Tambunam, the site of her next field visit, in 1967. She had not returned there since her 1938 excursion with Gregory Bateson. Mead made her second trip with Rhoda Metraux. The two anthropologists had lived together in New York City since 1955 and had collaborated on several books and research projects.

As their motor launch approached the village, Mead was filled with apprehension. She already knew that most of the villagers she had known had died, for "29 years is a long time in the lives of a people who die young." She also knew that the village had been bombed during World War II and that after the war a church and a school had been established. This meant, she feared, that the traditional ceremonial life of the Iatmul would be gone, replaced by Westernized ways. She did not know if any trace of the old Iatmul culture would remain.

In her 1938 book, *Letters from the Field*, Mead had termed Tambunam "the proudest and handsomest village on the river." But as she traveled up the Sepik River nearly three decades later, she reported feeling "rather as if I were hurrying to a deathbed, to record the death pangs of the Tambunams, once the fiercest, the proudest and most flamboyant people on the Sepik."

But Mead need not have worried. She noted with pleasure that "the pride of the Tambunam people is not broken." She was deeply impressed by the ways in which the Iatmul had managed to incorporate new customs into their culture without losing their traditions. "The old excitement of fighting and headhunting," she wrote, "had been replaced by a tremendous outburst of imaginative carving. The men have found a way, based on an old tradition, of reaching out into the modern world."

The villagers also reached out to Margaret Mead during her month-long stay. They set her up in a home situated near those of the friends she had made during her 1938 visit. The village elders eagerly reminisced with Mead about shared experiences. "In the evening," Mead said, "the men sit on boxes in the front part of the house and talk about the past. . . . They describe the night it rained on a crocodile hunt, when everyone rolled up the matting mosquito baskets and huddled in the wet darkness. They remember how Komankowi's baby was born with a tail (a bit of a membrane hanging on its back which I cut off) and tell me that he is now a married man with two children of his own."

Margaret Mead stands in the half-completed Hall of Pacific Peoples at New York's American Museum of Natural History.

Longtime companion Rhoda Metraux accompanied Mead on her return visit to the Iatmul village of Tambunam in 1967. The two anthropologists lived together in New York for more than 10 years.

Mead left Tambunam with a deep sense of satisfaction. She was pleased with the success the villagers were having in navigating the perilous transition into the modern age. And as an anthropologist, she was proud to document the past and present of these vigorous and warm New Guineans.

Between field visits Mead was often occupied with teaching. She gave courses at many colleges and universities, including Vassar, Stanford, Harvard, Emory, and Yale, but her main allegiance was to Columbia University in New York. The three courses she taught at Columbia during the spring semester of 1966 were typical of her academic schedule: "Cultures of the Pacific" and "Methods and Problems in Anthropology" were for undergraduates; the third, "Culture and Personality," was a graduate seminar. Mead's

95

Mead answers reporters' questions outside the UN World Population Conference in Bucharest, Romania, in 1974. The conference laid down guidelines for solving the world's socioeconomic problems.

brilliant mind and infectious energy inspired many young men and women to pursue careers in anthropology. Some of her protégés served as her teaching assistants at Columbia or staffed her office at the American Museum of Natural History.

When she was not teaching or working as a curator, Mead devoted time to an array of scientific organizations. She worked with the Institute for Intercultural Studies, which she had helped to found in 1944 with proceeds from her own and other anthropologists' book sales and speeches. The institute financed the fieldwork of talented young anthropologists. Mead also headed the World Foundation of Mental Health, and for three years she served as president of the prestigious American Association for the Advancement of Science.

Mead also continued to write. Alone or in collaboration with others, she published a total of more than 30 books, beginning in 1928 with *Coming of Age in Samoa* and ending with *World Enough: Rethinking the Future*, published in 1975. The titles of the volumes she wrote testify to the breadth of Mead's inquiring mind: *The Changing Culture of an Indian Tribe*, *Male and Female: A Study of the Sexes in a Changing World*, and *A Rap on Race*, which evolved from discussions between Mead and author James Baldwin. In addition, Mead contributed dozens of introductions to the books of other anthropologists, many of whom had been her students. Some of these books, said her daughter Mary Catherine Bateson (who became an anthropologist herself), "would never have been written except for the infusion of energy she gave."

Mead always seemed to be in the process of writing something. In addition to books, she contributed hundreds of articles to publications ranging from scholarly journals to popular newspapers. In 1961 she began writing a monthly column for the women's magazine *Redbook*. The column, which she would continue for the rest of her life, addressed topics such as "The Generation Gap," "Police and the Community," "Where American Women Are Now," and "Why Students Are Angry."

Because she wrote for the general public, Mead drew criticism from some scholars. She was accused of watering down "pure" anthropology by applying it to contemporary American life. But Mead did not agree. She believed that anthropology could—and should—be used to help people find their way in a complex world.

Mead wanted to give a taste of distant, fast-disappearing cultures—and the lessons they had taught her—to as many people as possible. She did this not only through her writing but also through her dedication to the new "Hall of the Peoples of the Pacific" that opened at the American Museum of Natural History in 1971. This was her hall; "It has been part of my own working life for 45 years," she once explained. Mead oversaw every aspect of work on the new hall, from inception through design and construction. Some of its exhibits—spears, carvings, bowls, and widows' capes—had been collected by the anthropologist herself during her expeditions to New Guinea and Bali. The creation of the hall appealed to Mead's desire for continuity and permanence. "Children who visit the Museum now," she said, "will one day bring their children to see how tapa cloth once was made or how people formerly lived in houses on stilts in an island lagoon."

Another way Mead brought anthropology to a wide audience was through public speaking. She enjoyed giving spontaneous talks and usually left her audiences mesmerized. She often discussed recent research and theories, but she also liked to shake up audiences with her outspoken opinions. A journalist in Oak Ridge, Tennessee, described one of Mead's more outrageous

Mead and Peri villager Paliau look through New Guinean artifacts and data in preparation for the 1971 opening of the Hall of Oceanic Peoples at the American Museum of Natural History.

performances: "This lady stood up there on the stage of the high school auditorium, looked a goodly percentage of the city's eggheads in the head, and suggested that, perhaps, they were a bunch of self-centered snobs."

Margaret Mead turned heads at private gatherings as well as at public meetings. At a 1960 party for her goddaughter, she slipped and broke her ankle. As she lay sprawled in pain on the floor, she asked one of the other guests, a photographer, to take a picture and record the moment for posterity. Her friend chivalrously refused, insisting that Mead did not look dignified. As Jane Howard reported in her biography of Mead, the injured anthropologist indignantly upbraided the photographer for lacking a sense of history, telling him he always missed "the important stuff."

While the indomitable Mead may have been unable to turn her broken ankle into a historical document, she was able to turn it into a personal statement. To support her healing ankle, Mead purchased a stylish forked walking stick, which she continued to use long after her injury healed. Mead wrote a friend that she planned to drape a trailing vine over the walking stick to dress up her look at parties. It would go well, she noted, with the grand, sweeping capes she had recently started to wear. This was a change for Mead, who was a practical woman who had always dressed suitably. As a young anthropologist in the field, she had donned light cotton dresses or native costumes. Now, as an established living legend,

she wore dramatic capes and wielded a formidable walking stick that gave her the air of a prophet.

Mead's convictions as an anthropologist, however, were much more down-to-earth. She believed that discoveries in her field could help improve people's lives. Accordingly, she got involved in a variety of causes in her later life. As a young woman, Mead had originally set out to help Franz Boas conduct a "giant rescue operation" to save the world's endangered cultures. In the 1960s and 1970s, she began to feel that an even more massive rescue operation was needed. "This time," Jane Howard wrote of Mead's view, "it was the planet that was imperiled, not just some disappearing distant peoples, and no one, in her view, could be exempt from helping with the task of salvation." Mead certainly did her part, speaking out for ecological responsibility and questioning dangerous technological developments such as nuclear arms and nuclear energy.

December 16, 1976, marked Margaret Mead's 75th birthday, an event that was news across the country. A celebration in her honor was held in Boston. Friends, admirers, and colleagues came out in force to pay tribute to one of the world's most brilliant and influential women. At the end of the all-day event, Mead noted that she had been treated "with extraordinary love and an enormous amount of undeserved praise . . . I ought to be embarrassed," she added, "and I'm not." When one reporter asked her if she planned to slow her pace in upcoming years, her re-

During her later years, Mead became involved in a number of social and political causes. She often spoke out against the nuclear arms race and ecological irresponsibility.

sponse was vintage Mead: "I expect to die, but I don't plan to retire."

Mead kept up her dizzying schedule the following year, traveling to Bali, Brazil, and Canada. She planned to visit the Soviet Union to research what her collaborator, Ken Heyman, called an "upbeat book" on aging. But in 1978, Mead received grim news: She had a malignant tumor on her pancreas. Increasingly ill and in terrible pain, she nonetheless continued to work as best she could. One of her friends noted that she "refused to live her life as if she were under the sentence of death." Mead finally succumbed to cancer on November 15, 1978, just a month before her 77th birthday.

Her death, and the many memorial services held for her, made headlines. Thousands of people, from college students to Polynesian villagers, from first ladies to Ash Can Cats, gathered to express their strong feelings about Margaret Mead. On January 20, 1979, the American Museum of Natural History held a special memorial service. Dignitaries and old friends packed the museum's auditorium. The crowd was so large that many people had to stand outside and watch the service on television monitors. The ceremony's highlight was the posthumous presentation of the Presidential Medal of Freedom, the highest award that can be bestowed on an American civilian in peacetime. Mary Catherine Bateson accepted her mother's medal, which was presented by UN ambassador Andrew Young on behalf of President Carter.

Mead devoted much of her life to the workings of the American Museum of Natural History (shown). Her office was located in the top portion of the tower on the left.

But perhaps the most touching tribute came from a tiny village thousands of miles from New York. When the residents of New Guinea's Peri village heard of Mead's passing, a week-long period of mourning was declared. The village council sent a telegram to the anthropologist's family: "People sorry of Margaret Mead's death. With sympathy, respect. Rested seven days. Planted coconut tree memory of great friend."

But not everyone saw Margaret Mead as a great friend; she did have professional adversaries, some of whom questioned the accuracy of her field reports. The strongest attack, one that once again propelled Mead's name into the headlines, came five years after her death. In 1983, Derek Freeman, an Australian anthropology professor, published a book challenging many of her conclusions about Samoa. In *Margaret Mead and Samoa: The Making and Unmaking of an Anthropological Myth*, Freeman charged that "Mead's account of Samoan culture and character is fundamentally in error."

In *Coming of Age in Samoa*, Mead had asserted that the residents of the Polynesian island passed easily into adulthood without the stresses associated with adolescence in the West. Her observations had bolstered the notion that culture, not biology, determined

When asked, on the occasion of her 75th birthday, if she would curtail her busy schedule, anthropologist Margaret Mead replied, "I expect to die, but I don't plan to retire."

many aspects of personality. Her conclusions affected social programs, science, and the way millions of people saw themselves. Now, more than a half century later, Freeman was saying that Mead had been wrong.

Based on historical research and his own fieldwork, Freeman maintained that Samoan adolescence, and Samoan culture in general, were far more troubled and complicated than Mead had depicted it to be. Some of the anthropologists interviewed in the wake of the controversy unleashed by Freeman's book speculated that Mead may have been duped by her Samoan informants. Others charged that she had not learned the Samoan language well enough to understand what those informants were saying to her.

But many social scientists—even those who agreed with some of Freeman's criticisms—supported Mead and *Coming of Age in Samoa*, the best-selling anthropology book of all time. When she began her career in the

1920s, Mead was simultaneously pioneering a discipline and trying to apply that discipline. The difficulties involved in carrying out this dual task may have distorted some of Mead's results, but they did not detract from the overall importance of her findings. Freeman himself came under considerable fire for waiting until after Mead's death to publish his book, because he thereby deprived her of the opportunity to defend herself. He was also criticized for comparing Mead's field site, a remote Samoan village in 1925, with the urbanized Samoan village he studied five decades later.

A balanced view of the Mead-Freeman controversy was voiced by Professor Bradd Shore of Emory University. Appearing on the "Donahue" television show along with Freeman and Mary Catherine Bateson, Shore stated that "Margaret Mead was not completely wrong on Samoa. . . . She was incomplete. And when someone is incomplete, you don't refute them, you correct, you add, and you also acknowledge what you have learned from them and what's—"

"That," interrupted Mary Catherine Bateson, "is called science."

And science, above all, was the passion of Margaret Mead's life. Not science practiced in an isolated laboratory or office but a science that was based on contact with humanity. None of Mead's innumerable friends, colleagues, and admirers had ever said that she made no mistakes or had no shortcomings. But nearly all agreed that she had earnestly set out to find out the truth: about cultures halfway around the world, about the best way to study these societies, and about ourselves.

Mead continually broke new ground. Single-handedly, she interested a wide audience in the emerging field of anthropology with her first book, *Coming of Age in Samoa*. And though she hesitated to label herself a feminist, she proved by her own example that women belonged, as much as men did, in the forefront of their chosen fields.

Margaret Mead caused people the world over to reexamine their values. In hundreds of books, articles, and speeches, she applied the lessons she had learned in the wilds of New Guinea and Bali to Western life. Probing the connection between society and individual personality, she urged people to look closely at their culture, for society shapes everything from childhood to sex roles. Her fondest hope, as she expressed it, was to build, "from a hundred cultures, one culture which does what no culture has ever done before—gives a place to every human gift." Mead's ultimate goal has yet to be realized, but she laid the groundwork that may make it possible for future generations to achieve this dream.

FURTHER READING

Bateson, Mary Catherine. *With a Daughter's Eye: A Memoir of Margaret Mead and Gregory Bateson.* New York: Morrow, 1984.

Freeman, Derek. *Margaret Mead and Samoa: The Making and Unmaking of an Anthropological Myth.* Cambridge: Harvard University Press, 1983.

Howard, Jane. *Margaret Mead: A Life.* New York: Simon & Schuster, 1984.

Mead, Margaret. *An Anthropologist at Work: Writings of Ruth Benedict.* New York: Houghton Mifflin, 1959.

———. *And Keep Your Powder Dry.* New York: Morrow, 1942.

———. *Blackberry Winter: My Earlier Years.* New York: Morrow, 1972.

———. *Coming of Age in Samoa: A Psychological Study of Primitive Youth for Western Civilization.* New York: Morrow, 1961 (originally published 1928).

———. *Growing up in New Guinea: A Comparative Study of Primitive Education.* New York: Morrow, 1930.

———. *Letters from the Field 1925–1975.* New York: Harper & Row, 1977.

———. *New Lives for Old: Cultural Transformation—Manus, 1928–1953.* New York: Morrow, 1956.

———. *Sex and Temperament in Three Primitive Societies.* New York: Morrow, 1935.

Mead, Margaret, and Ken Heyman. *Family.* New York: Macmillan, 1965.

Mead, Margaret, and Rhoda Metraux. *Aspects of the Present.* New York: Morrow, 1980.

CHRONOLOGY

Dec. 16, 1901	Margaret Mead born in Philadelphia, Pennsylvania
1918	Enrolls at DePauw University
1920	Transfers to Barnard College
1923	Graduates from Barnard; marries Luther Cressman; begins graduate work at Columbia University
1925–26	Conducts her first field trip, in American Samoa
1926	Becomes an assistant curator at the American Museum of Natural History
1928	Publishes *Coming of Age in Samoa*; divorces Cressman; marries Reo Fortune
1928–29	Carries out fieldwork with the Manus people of Peri Village, New Guinea
1930	Publishes *Growing up in New Guinea*; visits Nebraska to work with Omaha Indians
1930–33	Travels in New Guinea to study Arapesh, Mundugumor, and Tchambuli peoples
1935	Publishes *Sex and Temperament in Three Primitive Societies*
1936	Divorces Fortune; marries Gregory Bateson
1936–38	Conducts field trip in Bali, Indonesia
1938–39	Visits Iatmul people in Tambunam, New Guinea
1939	Gives birth to Mary Catherine Bateson
1942	Publishes *And Keep Your Powder Dry*
1950	Divorces Bateson
1953	Makes a return field trip to Peri Village
1960	Publishes *New Lives for Old*
1964	Visits Peri Village a third time
1967	Returns to Tambunam, New Guinea
1971	Opens the Hall of the Peoples of the Pacific at the American Museum of Natural History
1972	Publishes *Blackberry Winter*
Nov. 15, 1978	Margaret Mead dies in New York, New York

INDEX

Abelam, 60
Adams, Leonie, 37
Admiralty Islands, 51–52
Adolescence, 14, 16, 18, 43, 47–49, 54, 101
Aibom, New Guinea, 65
Alitoa, New Guinea, 60, 63
Ambunti, New Guinea, 64
American Association for the Advancement of Science, 96
American Museum of Natural History, 39, 51, 55, 57, 60, 69, 71, 83, 96–97, 100
American Samoa, 13–15, 17–19, 20, 22, 43, 47–49, 51, 101–3
And Keep Your Powder Dry, 82–83
Anthropology, 13–14, 19, 21, 37–39, 41–42, 49, 51, 71, 97
Arapesh. *See* Mountain Arapesh
Ash Can Cats, 36–37, 100
Awayness, 79

Bajoeng Gede, Indonesia, 73, 75
Baldwin, James, 97
Bali, Indonesia, 71–73, 75–76, 78–79, 91, 97, 100, 103
Balinese, 73
Balinese Character: A Photographic Analysis, 75, 82
Bangli, Indonesia, 75
Barnard College, 35–38, 42

Bateson, Gregory, 65, 69, 71–73, 75–79, 81–84, 93
Bateson, Mary Catherine, 81, 84, 97, 102–3
Batoean, Indonesia, 75
Benedict, Ruth Fulton, 40–41, 57, 71
Blackberry Winter, 14, 28–29, 33–34, 36, 38–41, 47, 51, 59, 63, 68, 81
Boas, Franz, 14, 38–43, 47, 68, 99
Brazil, 100
British Association for the Advancement of Science, 42
Brooke, Rupert, 13
Bryn Mawr College, 24
Buckingham Valley, Pennsylvania, 27

Cambridge University, 51, 69
Canada, 100
Cargo cults, 85
Carter, Jimmy, 100
Changing Culture of an Indian Tribe, The, 60, 97
Chicago, University of, 23
City College, 51
Clark University, 39
Cockfights, 75
Columbia University, 14, 36, 39, 42, 51, 55, 60, 71, 83, 95–96
Coming of Age in Samoa: A Psychological Study of Primitive Youth for Western Civilization, 19,

21, 48–49, 51, 55, 97, 101–3
Committee on National Morale, 83
Cressman, Luther, 13, 29, 36, 41–42, 47, 51

DePauw University, 31, 33–35
Doylestown, Pennsylvania, 29

Emory University, 95, 102

Fale, 17
Family, 91
First Days in the Life of a New Guinea Baby, 82
Fitiuta, American Samoa, 19
Fortune, Reo, 51–57, 59–60, 62–65, 68–69, 71, 84, 92–93
Frank, Larry, 84
Frank, Mary, 84
Freeman, Derek, 101–3

General Theological Seminary, 41
Germany, 39, 51
Great Britain, 47, 51
Great Depression, 55
Growing Up in New Guinea, 52, 57

Hall of the Peoples of the Pacific, 97
Hammonton, New Jersey, 27
Harvard University, 95

INDEX

Heyman, Ken, 91, 100
Hitler, Adolf, 75, 83
Holmquist School, 29
Holt, Edward, 17–18
Howard, Jane, 57, 99

Iatmul, 76–79, 93–95
I Madé Kaler, 73
Institute of Cultural Studies, 96

Journal of the American Statistical Association, 42

Kankanamun, New Guinea, 64
Kawas, 53
Kenakatem, New Guinea, 63–64
Kilipak, 54, 86
Komankowi, 94
Kutan, 86

Latham, Minor W., 36
Letters from the Field, 59, 93
Lila, 17–18
Luma, American Samoa, 17–18

Malaria, 54
Malay, 73
Male and Female: A Study of the Sexes in a Changing World, 97
Manus (people), 52–54, 84–89, 91–95
Manus, New Guinea, 52, 84–89, 91–95
Manus Religion (Fortune), 57
Manuwai, 87
Margaret Mead: A Life (Howard), 57, 99
Margaret Mead and Samoa: The Making and Unmaking of an Anthropological Myth (Freeman), 101

Maugham, Somerset, 15
Mead, Catherine (sister), 24, 81
Mead, Edward Sherwood (father), 13, 23–24, 26–29, 31, 43
Mead, Elizabeth (sister), 24
Mead, Emily Fogg (mother), 23–24, 26–27, 31, 81
Mead, Margaret,
  in Bali, 71–73, 75–79, 91, 97, 100
  early years, 23–29, 31, 33–41
  examines American society, 82–83
  gives birth, 81
  her findings challenged, 101–3
  honored, 100–101
  late field trips of, 91–95
  later years and death of, 91–97, 99–100
  marries, 41, 51, 71
  in Nebraska, 57, 59–60
  in New Guinea, 52–55, 60–68, 76–78, 84–89, 91–95, 97
  religious beliefs of, 28–29
  in Samoa, 13–15, 17–19, 20, 22, 43, 45, 47
Mead, Martha Ramsay (grandmother), 24–25, 81
Mead, Priscilla (sister), 24
Mead, Richard (brother), 24
Melanesia, 85
Metraux, Rhoda, 93
Minority, The, 34
Mountain Arapesh, 60–64, 66, 68
Mundugumor, 63–66, 68

National Research Council, 15, 43, 51, 83
Nebraska, 57, 59
New Guinea, 51–55, 60–68, 71, 73, 76–78, 84–89, 91–95, 97, 101, 103

New Hope, Pennsylvania, 29
New Lives for Old, 89
New York, New York, 36, 42, 51, 55, 60, 69, 81, 83, 93
New Zealand, 51
Nineteenth Amendment, 36

Oak Ridge, Tennessee, 97, 99
Omaha Indians, 57, 59–60
Omaha Secret Societies (Fortune), 60

Pago Pago, American Samoa, 14–15, 17
Pennsylvania, University of, 23
Peri, New Guinea, 52, 54, 84–89, 92–93, 101
Philadelphia, Pennsylvania, 13–14, 23, 27, 29
Pidgin English, 52, 83
Poepoe, 73
Pokanau, 92
Polynesia, 42–43, 47, 51

Racial determination, 39, 43
"Rain" (Maugham), 15
Rap on Race, A, 97
Redbook, 97
Rivers, William, 19
Rothenberger, Katharine, 34–35

San Francisco, California, 13
Schizophrenia, 71–72, 79
Schwartz, Lenora, 84
Schwartz, Theodore, 84
Sepik River, 76, 93
Sex and Temperament in Three Primitive Societies, 69, 71
Sex roles, 60–64, 66–68, 103
Shore, Bradd, 102–3
Sorcerers of Debu (Fortune), 57
Sori, 54
Sororities, 33–35

Soviet Union, 100
Stanford University, 95
Stevenson, Robert Louis, 13, 35

Taboos, 73, 75, 85
Talala, 19
Tambaran, 60–61
Tambunam, New Guinea, 76, 93–95
Tau, American Samoa, 17–19, 47–48
Tchambuli (people), 65–68

Tchambuli, New Guinea, 65–68
Torricelli Mountains, 60
Trance and Dance in Bali, 82
Tusitala, 35
Tutuila, American Samoa, 14

Ufuti, 17

Vaitogi, American Samoa, 15, 17
Vassar College, 95

Washington, D.C., 83
Wellesley College, 31
Wissler, Clark, 57
With a Daughter's Eye (Bateson), 84
World Enough: Rethinking the Future, 97
World Foundation of Mental Health, 96
World War I, 29
World War II, 82–85, 93

Yale University, 95

Edra Ziesk, a free-lance writer based in New York City, has published both fiction and nonfiction pieces in a wide variety of magazines, newspapers, and literary journals. Her work has appeared in *Working Woman, Family Circle, Other Voices, Plainswoman,* and numerous other periodicals.

Matina S. Horner is president of Radcliffe College and associate professor of psychology and social relations at Harvard University. She is best known for her studies of women's motivation, achievement, and personality development. Dr. Horner serves on several national boards and advisory councils, including those of the National Science Foundation, Time Inc., and the Women's Research and Education Institute. She earned her B.A. from Bryn Mawr College and Ph.D. from the University of Michigan, and holds honorary degrees from many colleges and universities, including Mount Holyoke, Smith, Tufts, and the University of Pennsylvania.